pure and simple

taste

taste
pure and simple

irresistible recipes for good food and good health

by **michel nischan** with **mary goodbody**

FOREWORD BY DREW NIEPORENT
PHOTOGRAPHS BY MINH + WASS

CHRONICLE BOOKS
SAN FRANCISCO

dedication

For my mother, Esther, whose love of life and homespun common sense taught me that many of life's lessons can be learned through the simple act of slicing a cucumber. Her unwavering love for pleasing others is the purest form of genuine hospitality. So many of my memories come from and lead back to her cooking. I pray this book does her proud.

acknowledgments

Text copyright © 2003 by Michel Nischan.
Photographs copyright © 2003 by Minh + Wass.
All rights reserved. No part of this book
may be reproduced in any form
without written permission from the publisher.

Library of Congress
Cataloging-in-Publication Data available.

ISBN 0-8118-3377-1

Manufactured in China.

DESIGN BY JULIA FLAGG
PROP STYLING BY NGOC MINH NGO
FOOD STYLING BY SUSIE THEODOROU

The photographers wish to thank the chef,
Michel Nishan, for entrusting us to represent
his wonderful creations; Susie Theodorou
for making the food look so beautiful; and
Takashimaya Department Store for the
exquisite ceramics.

Distributed in Canada by Raincoast Books
9050 Shaughnessy Street
Vancouver, British Columbia V6P 6E5

2 4 6 8 10 9 7 5 3

Chronicle Books LLC
85 Second Street
San Francisco, California 94105

www.chroniclebooks.com

My wife, Lori, has always given me the love and support only a true soul mate can, including the unbridled, spot-on criticism that has made me a better person, a better father, and a better chef. I thank her for making my life so very amazing and for keeping me on the right track.

My brave son, Chris, deals daily with the painful realities of type 1 diabetes. His ability to handle the setbacks of such a devastating disease is the true impetus that changed my cooking. Each of my five children has given me something special. They all give me hope for great things to come. I'm a lucky guy.

Sheila Margulis is the glue that kept my professional life together since I embarked on my journey of heathful cooking. She has brought a semblance of order to my life. For the numerous monthly events, from interviews, personal appearances, special dinners, and menu changes to accommodating the likes of Dalai Lama and Amazonian Shaman (not to mention lost keys and forgotten phone numbers!), Sheila has monitored every detail.

Mark, Liliana, and all the good people at the Amazon Conservation Team (ACT) possess an unwavering ability to literally move mountains against impossible odds. This makes their visions a reality and continues to lead me. Taita Luciano, I hear you. Thank you. ACT is a grassroots organization that works to preserve the cultures and homelands of indigenous peoples throughout tropical America.

Nora Pouillon decided to open the first certified-organic restaurant in the United States, Nora's, in Washington, D.C. Her courage, foresight, and wisdom are difficult to match. I thought of her often when building my own organic lifestyle.

Mary Goodbody helped me write this book in a way that allowed me to be me and she to be she. She "got it" when I spoke about food and didn't edit me to make me sound like someone I am not. Her experience and professionalism kept this book on track, and made it a book well worth reading. Let's do more!

My agent, Jane Dystel, convinced me that this idea "will" make a good book, and "this is what it should be called." She is an exceptional advisor and advocate who possesses a tremendous sense of integrity.

Fern Berman and Laura Lehrman of Fern Berman Communications believe that what we are doing is special and deserves attention. They saw that we got the attention. Fern believed there was a book in this new cuisine and moved things forward by introducing me to Jane Dystel.

Here's to the loyalty and humor of John Mooney and Mike Fichtel, the sous chefs at my two former restaurants. Neither this book nor the restaurants would have been possible without John's and Mike's dedication and high level of execution. John and the Heartbeat crew came to our kitchen never having worked in a place that didn't sauté in butter, mount with goose fat, bathe in foie gras, or simmer in cream. They accepted the challenge as interesting and inspiring, and added their own personalities.

Drew Nieporent is the greatest restaurateur in the world because he does everything for the absolute right reason. His sense of humanity runs uncommonly deep, and he has done many great things for me and many others—all by simply being himself. The restaurant industry would look entirely different today if not for his countless contributions. Drew saw the opportunity and need for a restaurant like Heartbeat and made it happen. No one else could have.

Michael Bonadies is the unsung giant of the Myriad Restaurant Group. He selflessly travels about the country keeping our many projects and careers on track—including mine. Michael convinced me that I could open my debut restaurant in Manhattan without butter and foie gras. For me, he is the "advisor general."

Tracy Nieporent, Drew's brother, has always been there for me . . . always. The term "unwavering friendship" has taken on new meaning because of him. I'd say more, but don't need to.

Bernie Shimmerman, my only true mentor, taught me that to be a good chef I had to be a good manager, a good cook, and still have a good laugh. He was the first, other than my wife, Lori, who truly believed in me. There were many hard lessons I didn't particularly like, but in the end Bernie's lessons were good ones. God rest your wonderful soul.

My grandmother Amelia Nischan "learned" my mom how to "really fry chicken" and taught three generations of Nischans how to love through food. I can still taste the love. Thanks, Granny.

My dad told me the only way I would make it in life was if I could sell myself. The tough part, he said, would be in making the product worth selling. Dad didn't live to see me come as far as I have but I have thrived on that advice, which took me a lifetime to listen to. Dad, you were right. I'm sorry. I miss and love you. Thank you.

table of contents

foreword 8

introduction 9

appetizers and salads

summer melons with ginger 22

oven-roasted tomatoes with goat cheese and
    extra-virgin olive oil 23

sautéed scallops with creamy corn sauce 24

tamari shrimp and scallops 27

sashimi of fluke with sweet shrimp 28

fresh oysters with ginger-sake mignonette 30

white bean dip 31

asian pear salad with tamari pecans and
    maytag blue cheese 33

tamari pecans 34

roasted root vegetables and baby greens salad 35

heirloom tomato salad with aged balsamic vinaigrette 37

fresh tuna and radish salad with wasabi dressing 38

soups

sweet corn and vegetable chowder 42

heirloom tomato soup 45

green tomato soup with heirloom tomatoes and
    vidalia onion garnish 47

heirloom squash soup with roasted chestnuts 48

black-eyed pea soup with wilted greens 49

basmati and black rice juk 51

pan-toasted garlic and wilted spinach soup 52

celery root and truffle soup 53

fish and shellfish

spicy grilled snapper with ginger and lemongrass 56

roasted monkfish with porcini mushrooms
    and fava beans 59

sautéed halibut with celery root and truffle 61

miso salmon with english pea sauce 62

cured salmon with caramelized cauliflower 64

pan-roasted cod with celery and heirloom potatoes 67

steamed black bass with kombu noodles and
    mushroom dashi 69

crab cakes with papaya and jicama salad 70

grilled prawns with fennel and onions 71

poultry and **meats**

pistachio-roasted poussin 74

roasted chicken breasts with dinosaur plum sauce 76

chicken and grilled-corn succotash 77

pan-roasted chicken with heirloom tomatoes and
    fresh bay leaves 78

roast turkey with sweet potato gravy and
    heirloom squash dressing 80

roast capon with napa cabbage and autumn pears 84

pan-roasted quail with peach and porcini
    mushroom hash 87

coriander breast of duck with sweet potato sauce 88

mustard-roasted tenderloin of pork with
    rutabaga and golden beets 91

grilled leg of lamb with cherries, rhubarb, and
    horseradish 94

rack of lamb with pomegranate-date chutney 96

natural beef tenderloin with wild mushrooms and
    yukon gold potatoes 99

garlic-grilled strip steak with corn béarnaise 101

bison "cube" steak with fresh figs **103**

marinated venison loin steaks with onions and
    sweet peppers **104**

vegetarian entrées

sweet potato and root vegetable gratin **108**

winter vegetable stew **110**

sweet pea, corn, and mushroom risotto **113**

roasted vegetables with sweet corn and
    fire-roasted sweet pepper sauce **115**

vegetable lasagne **116**

side dishes

grilled summer peppers with fresh bay leaves **120**

grilled asparagus **122**

"marshmallow" corn **123**

garlic mashed potatoes **124**

root vegetable and wild mushroom hash **125**

lightly salted edamame **127**

garlic wilted spinach **128**

"wok"-charred bok choy **129**

breakfast

squash pancakes with fig syrup **133**

breakfast vegetable hash **134**

steel-cut oatmeal with apricots and mission figs **135**

pastel omelet with shiitake mushrooms, goat cheese,
    and fresh herbs **137**

granola **138**

dessert

fresh figs with semolina toast and rhododendron honey **142**

flourless hazelnut cakes with chocolate centers **144**

almond polenta cake with orange cream **146**

champagne mangos with raspberry coulis and
    cardamom shortbread **148**

cardamom shortbread **150**

sweet potato brûlée **151**

basics

creamy corn sauce **156**

fire-roasted sweet pepper sauce **156**

buttermilk sour cream **157**

raw sugar simple syrup **157**

red or golden beet syrup **157**

rutabaga syrup **158**

pear syrup **158**

grilled corn **158**

shelled fava beans **158**

roasted garlic **159**

roasted garlic cloves **159**

roasted garlic stock **159**

spring garlic stock **160**

rich chicken stock **160**

chicken glaze **161**

rich beef or veal stock **161**

ham hock stock **162**

rich fish stock **162**

roasted vegetable stock **163**

simple vegetable stock **164**

roasted corn stock **164**

rich mushroom stock **165**

huitlacoche sauce **165**

juicing fruits and vegetables **166**

roasting vegetables **166**

glossary **167**

mail-order sources **171**

index **172**

table of equivalents **175**

foreword

The first time I met Michel Nischan, I was immediately impressed with his warmth and sincerity. As Corporate Consulting Chef at my company, the Myriad Restaurant Group, Michel impressed everyone with his work ethic and enthusiasm. He created a great working environment and made everyone around him better. My brother, Tracy, who is our Director of Marketing, was always remarking to me how enthusiastic and cooperative Michel was in fulfilling media requests and participating in charitable events. I don't know how many times I heard him say, "Michel is a pleasure to work with. He loves what he does and it shows. He gets it."

Tracy is right. Michel is passionate and totally devoted to excellence. Great chefs have to be. Like many talented chefs, he also has an ego, but it's not directed to self-promotion. Rather, it's devoted to the betterment of his craft, to making his co-workers more effective, to satisfying our guests.

For a long time, I had wanted to create a restaurant that broke new ground by serving substantial, indulgent food that didn't include butter, heavy cream, or any saturated fat. I wanted to blaze a new trail with a concept that was important, substantial, and indeed, necessary for our times. But a concept cannot live without a chef who can articulate it and bring it to life. Michel embraced the assignment with tremendous energy and a sense of mission. He did extensive research, experimented diligently, and through exhaustive trial and error, developed the menu that became the essence of Heartbeat.

I am proud of what Michel has accomplished. As you read the pages of this book and try these recipes, you will become a believer. A whole new way of enjoying food awaits you. It's a meaningful journey on which you are embarking.

The discovery begins as you turn these pages. Bon Appetit!

introduction

I never intended the pursuit of healthful, organic cooking to be my lifelong endeavor, much less my passion. But I am passionate about it: passionate about achieving balance in every meal, about eating what is ripe and best in its season, and about enjoying the pure pleasure of eating simply and well.

Make no mistake, this is not a "health-food" book. My recipes are not overloaded with whole grains, tofu, and legumes. I cook all of these foods—and appreciate them—but I also cook delicate seafood, robust red meat, and chocolaty desserts. My method is to allow the base ingredient to shine in its full glory. Corn is all about corn, sweet peas are about sweet peas, and so on. I use healthful techniques such as steaming and poaching. I adjust less healthful methods, like sautéing, by varying pan temperature and choosing oils, such as canola, that can withstand high heat without breaking down. I use extra-virgin olive oil for its great flavor and versatility—although it cannot be used in high-heat cooking, since it breaks down when its temperature gets too high. This kind of cooking relies on pristine stocks (made with bones only) and juices to achieve sauces that are pure in flavor and naturally balanced without excess seasoning and fat.

Nothing here is complicated, although some recipes require more time than others. A juicer is the only piece of equipment you will need that is not found in most well-appointed home kitchens. Once you integrate one of these powerful machines into your kitchen, it will become as familiar and convenient to use as a food processor. No need to buy the most expensive or elaborate juicer on the market, but you should buy a reliable one that will last

for years. Look for a juicer that is capable of juicing a good amount of produce and is easy to clean. As you juice, pulp accumulates in a strainer, which must be cleaned after every use with cool running water. I particularly like the Braun juicer.

On these pages, you will find techniques and ideas that may be unusual, even foreign. Believe me, they were uncharted territory for me, too, both when I was the chef at Heartbeat from 1998 to 2002 and now, as I teach others to cook healthfully and organically.

MY JOURNEY

I have not always been interested in healthful cooking. I was raised on Southern country cooking (read: soul food) and then trained as a chef in Continental and French restaurants. The first restaurant I owned, Miche Mache in Norwalk and then Stamford, Connecticut, featured a blending of the various styles of cooking that reflected my background and training. The menu included plenty of dishes that relied on fat, which is not surprising considering my culinary heritage.

My mother was raised in Missouri on a Depression-era farm where she and my grandmother cooked for a huge family. They grew their own vegetables, slaughtered and cured their own meat, and even took their wheat to a local mill to be ground into flour. Later, when she had a family of her own, Mom retained much of her early connection to the land and the kind of cooking she knew.

Mom was an excellent cook and, as a child, I spent many hours with her in her kitchen and extensive garden. The act of cooking intrigued me, especially because the end result tasted so good! Something a growing boy could appreciate.

I learned about hospitality, too, from my mother. If one tomato was larger than another, she offered our guest the larger one. If there were only a few watermelon pickles or banana peppers left in the jar, Mom opened a new jar for guests. When she cooked for company, I'd catch her giggling quietly as she added an extra handful of herbs or some other little touch. "They're going to love this!" she would say with a smile.

Our diet was one of smothered pork chops, fried chicken, ham and eggs, and cornmeal-coated catfish. Doesn't sound too healthy, does it? But with every meal, Mom served three, four, or five cooked or raw vegetables: simmered cauliflower, skillet broccoli, collard greens, black-eyed peas, pole beans, leaf lettuce salad, sliced tomatoes, corn on the cob, and so much more. These vegetables balanced every meal and I realize now that no single cuisine, not even Southern country, is unhealthful. It's our own eating habits that sabotage our diets.

From dining out with friends as well as from cooking for restaurant customers, I have come to understand why we Americans tend to be overweight and often unhealthy. For example, when friends and I eat at country-style restaurants, like those I grew up with in the Midwest, I select an entrée and then ask for a side of greens, beans, okra, or some other veggie. My friends order fried chicken with mashed potatoes, macaroni and cheese, and fried hush puppies! Given the choice, most Americans gladly eat a horribly unbalanced diet. Restaurateurs recognize this, and so menus at fast-food drive-throughs and upscale restaurants alike are geared toward indulgent foods. In every fine-dining restaurant where I have worked, butter, cream, cheese, and foie gras are used with near abandon. And often a diner has no choice about what is served with an entrée.

FICKLE CUSTOMERS AND FAT

I built my career by staying on the move and keeping my nose to the cutting board. My first job was at a truck stop in northern Illinois, but armed with Mom's high standards, I eventually landed in the kitchens of some of the best French restaurants in Chicago.

French methodology amazed me. My mother always saved fat—beef, chicken, pork, bacon—for cooking, but when I entered a French kitchen I learned to cook with butter and expensive oils. The French "mount" sauces with fat, usually butter. This means they thicken and smooth their sauces by adding small amounts of fat during cooking, letting the fat emulsify rather than melt, and then add more until the sauce achieves the velvety texture and superrich flavor that have made French sauces famous the world over.

I embraced this technique wholeheartedly, and then decided to expand it by mounting beef-based sauces with beef fat, chicken-based sauces with chicken fat, and so on. By the time I opened Miche Mache in 1991, I had perfected my technique and was experimenting with various fats and foods. For instance, I made a confit of baby goat with a combination of bacon and goose fat infused with roasted garlic, cardamom, and fresh bay leaves. I poached lobsters in olive oil flavored with vanilla and Meyer lemon. I was having a great time going slightly crazy with fat.

Regardless of the vats of fat in the kitchen, I always treated vegetables with reverence. Every entrée was served with at least two vegetables and often no starches. I found customers rearranging their orders to include a starch instead of a vegetable or foregoing the veggies altogether and ordering two starches. This troubled me, but as a chef I believe in giving customers what they want.

Another type of customer troubled me equally. These were the weekly regulars who always ordered the same chicken or fish dish. Boring! When I changed the menu, these customers walked back to the kitchen and begged me to reinstate their favorites. Of course, I did.

After Miche Mache had been open for three years, my wife, Lori, and I learned that our five-year-old son Chris had type-1 diabetes. The news rocked our world and changed our family life forever. The doctors made it clear that the relationship between Chris's diet and his overall health was crucial both for his daily well-being and for his life expectancy.

By this time, Lori and I knew about 80 percent of our customers at Miche Mache. Lori is a gregarious, intelligent, attractive, and unbelievably hospitable woman, and many of our customers knew about our family, just as we knew about theirs. Word about Chris's illness spread among them, and the outpouring of support was heart-warming and reassuring. Many also shared their own health problems. Who knew? Many of our regulars had diabetes, heart disease, liver and blood disorders. The list went on. These turned out to be those same "boring customers" who always ordered the same safe fish and chicken dishes.

OPENING A MENU CAN BE DEPRESSING

The fact that so many of my friends and customers had health problems was an eye-opener for me. Combined with what I was learning about my son's illness and its link to diet, I was determined to offer dishes on the menu that would be healthful and delicious.

It had never crossed my mind that so many people faced the daily challenges of a restricted diet. They might be passionate about food—so many of our Miche Mache customers were—but when they opened a restaurant menu, they had to consider what they could not eat instead of enjoying the fun of choosing at will. They worked hard to rearrange the menu so that they could eat the food without inconveniencing the kitchen.

Sure, there are plenty of restaurant diners who have no qualms about making special requests and at the same time drive the kitchen staff nuts. However, I was finding that nine out of ten times, my customers hated having to ask for special attention and were embarrassed about the fuss and bother.

Something had to be done. I overreacted at first, cringing every time I poached fish in seasoned pork fat or used bacon and goose fat to mount a popular sauce. I even had nightmares about customers being rushed to the hospital after eating my food!

After a few anxious months, I achieved some balance, both in my family life and at the restaurant. Out went all the junk food at home and in came fruits and vegetables and bottled water. At work, a similar, albeit partial, purging took place. I researched healthful oils, which turned me on to grapeseed oil, and I drastically cut back on the amount of animal fat I used in sauces. Vegetables became even more important on the menu, just as they had been on my mother's table when I was growing up and learning about food.

FEAR OF THE NEW AND DIFFERENT

Even as we changed a number of items on our menu at Miche Mache, I was painfully aware of how unusual this was among upscale restaurants. At this time in the early 1990s, fat was in—with a vengeance. It was chic to revolt against the "food police"—and in truth the politically correct rhetoric went too far. The state of New Jersey made it against the law to serve over-easy eggs for fear of salmonella poisoning. Getting anything but a dry, overcooked burger was next to impossible nearly everywhere, and beautiful artisan food imports were banned from the United States in record numbers.

I remember reading how annoyed Julia Child was by all this hoopla. She stressed the importance of fat in everyone's diet, and insisted that moderation was the best policy. I agree. Fat holds an irreplaceable role in most cuisines, and while we should be guided by as much accurate information as we can get, how we cook must be a personal choice.

The problem was (and still is today) there were not enough choices for restaurant customers hoping to reduce fat. Numerous food writers and critics stirred the pot with their own point of view by demonizing anyone attempting to serve healthful food. Clearly, a chef with any sense would run screaming from the idea of opening a restaurant that focused on it.

This included me. I was deeply motivated to step into the fray and offer healthful foods but I was also scared to death. In the end, Miche Mache continued to rely a great deal on fat, although we had specially designed dishes on the menu for anyone concerned about diet.

GREAT MINDS GET THINGS DONE

I limped along like this for a while, worrying that I was not doing enough but also content to help my customers when I could. The turning point in my career came when I met Drew Nieporent and Michael Bonadies, partners in Myriad Restaurant Group and responsible for some of the world's best and most respected restaurants: Montrachet, Layla, and Tribeca Grill in New York; Nobu in New York and London; and Rubicon in San Francisco.

Drew has an unparalleled love for life and a passion for all kinds of good food; he also is a wellspring of ideas. Michael has an equally amazing culinary mind. I closed Miche Mache, went to work for Drew as a corporate consulting chef, and opened several hotel restaurants for clients. During these three years, I had an ongoing discussion with Michael about having my own kitchen again. The opportunity arose when Drew and Michael began working with Starwood Hotels and Resorts, Worldwide (then called Starwood Lodging Corporation). The company proposed opening a Manhattan hotel with a restaurant to match the "urban oasis" concept for the rest of the hotel, which included a spa, gyms, and serene guest rooms. The hotel was named the W New York. Drew suggested calling the restaurant Heartbeat; he also suggested I take it on.

My head was spinning with ideas. I was being asked to open a debut restaurant in New York, the culinary capital of the world. What could be more thrilling and a better opportunity? Then Drew told me his concept meant creating a menu that used no butter, cream, or saturated fat. I was terrified. What would the sophisticated New York dining public make of this?

Despite my fears, Drew wisely insisted on the premise. I resigned myself to hanging on a long, thin branch over a fast-moving river, with my own long, thin neck sticking out even farther! What I didn't realize was that I would quickly fulfill my own strong convictions, which would anchor me during the frenzy that always surrounds opening a new restaurant.

STAY CLOSE TO HOME; BANISH THE DEMONS

Drew's vision kept us focused on what Heartbeat should be while Michael focused on saving me from myself. "Stay close to home," he advised when I voiced apprehension and doubt. "Remember the roots of your mother's cooking and her reverence for food. Think about a perfect tomato. Think about the farmers and their produce. Think about your contribution to the culinary world."

We talked long and hard about the idea of Heartbeat and my anxiety about creating a menu that reflected Drew's vision. Quite honestly, I was concerned that New Yorkers would not know what to make of us, and by association, of me. I was about to open an upscale restaurant without an ounce of foie gras in sight!

Again, Michael's calm words worked for me. "Is this all about you and your ego?" he asked. "Or is this about what you hope to accomplish for the dining public?"

I dug inside myself and banished the demons of ego. I thought about my son, Chris, my former customers at Miche Mache, and Drew's vision. As simply and predictably as the sun rises over a farmer's fields, everything lined up with surety. I understood our destiny: Heartbeat, regardless of how well it was accepted and appreciated, was meant to happen.

I immersed myself in the kitchen. I realized that without cream and butter, my sauce arsenal would be severely limited, but when I recalled the work I had done with various fruit and vegetable juices, I thought of using them to finish sauces and broths. Following a hunch, I juiced starch-laden vegetables such as sweet potatoes and corn and then heated them to see if they would thicken on their own, without the addition of processed starch (like cornstarch or flour). I began having successes.

I looked to Asia for powerful flavor statements made with few ingredients. I experimented with low-temperature sautéing to prevent oil from breaking down over high heat and converting into free radicals. I worked with seasoned steaming broths, citrus zests, short-term brines, and long, slow roasting. I bathed in grapeseed oil and showered in citrus!

I stayed close to home, a decision that took me down the road to serving as much organically raised produce as humanly possible in a big-city hotel. I hired the best person I knew to help me find the finest produce available. Chett Abramson and I had worked together at Tribeca Grill, and I knew he was capable of locating just about anything I needed. This was crucial to the concept of the restaurant. For example, if sweet potato juice is going to be 98 percent of a sauce, the raw sweet potato had better be as good as it can be. If it is tasteless, the sauce will be tasteless.

With Chett's help, we established relationships with some of the best farmers and purveyors in the country. These are folks who care enough about flavor and the earth to raise fruits, vegetables, and animals organically and naturally. They look at food as life rather than a commodity.

A SHAKY START TO SMOOTH SAILING

In three months, I had developed only six appetizers and eight entrees—not enough to open. I hired Brian Wheeler (now executive chef at Layla restaurant in New York), John Mooney, and Joel Hough to help me come up with enough dishes so that we could open on time. We pushed ourselves and each other and were ready when the restaurant was scheduled to open in the fall of 1998. A few of these dishes are in this book, including Tamari Shrimp and Scallops (page 27), Asian Pear Salad (page 33), and Coriander Breast of Duck with Sweet Potato Sauce (page 88).

Before that could happen, I had to hire and train staff. As I began, I was struck with a terrifying thought: No one had ever cooked food like this "on the line" for restaurant service. Not even the four of us. Would it work?

Luckily, the staff shared our vision and passion and had a genuine desire to learn something different. Still, no matter how willing everyone was to learn and work hard, we had our share of disasters to go with our successes. Sauces broke, and we had to cook them in small batches in double boilers. Some had to be started several times over in a single night.

The press was relatively kind, although we had our share of misses as well as hits. Customers were complimentary, but I couldn't help feel at times the praise was lukewarm. We scrambled for six months before we hit our stride—but hit it we did. The key was in relaxing. We were trying way too hard and not letting the ingredients speak for themselves. Once Drew helped us recognize this, we allowed these amazing ingredients to do the work for us. We kept the food pure and simple. Almost overnight, everything changed. People started to refer to dishes as "amazing" instead of "good." Culinary professionals who visited our kitchen took note of the difference in our cooking and appreciated the rhythm and order necessary for nightly success. New dishes came naturally, with ideas emanating from the entire staff and especially John and Joel.

We had reached the promised land of a new cuisine. Everyone felt it, from our staff to our customers, and it was a very good feeling. What's more, it was and remains a privilege.

A WORD ON SAUCES

Sauce is the banner of the world's great cuisines and I look to French and Asian chefs for inspiration. For generations chefs around the world have taken cues from the French.

Several classic French sauces, such as béchamel and espagnol, begin with a roux (a cooked combination of flour and butter). Today, modern-thinking French chefs rely more on reductions and purées than roux. But they still use cream and butter to give many of their sauces balance and that irresistible silken texture.

Asian cuisines boast an arsenal of sauces, but few are as famous as the French—though I predict that's about to change. Asian sauces are thin and powerfully seasoned, made with ingredients such as soy, fish sauce, mirin, citrus juice, and rice vinegar. If an Asian sauce is thickened at all, it is thickened with cornstarch.

When I owned Miche Mache, I did it all. I made roux with various animal fats. I mounted sauces with them and even used leftover scraps of foie gras to flavor sauces. I used cream reductions as the base for a number of sauces and occasionally finished some with whipped cream. I was in sauce heaven—until I realized I was unintentionally harming people.

As I have said, before we opened Heartbeat, I started experimenting with juices to make sauces. I was dedicated to the notion of serving intriguing sauces, which are so important to any dish because, other than their all-important flavor, they provide dimension, color, interest, comfort, and moisture.

I first thought of vegetables with natural starch content, such as potatoes, sweet potatoes, corn, and winter squash. Sweet potato was my first choice. I juiced it, cooked it, and saw that it thickened immediately. Then I tasted it. There was so much starch in it my tongue puckered, and the unpleasant flavor of the raw starch hit me like a board on the side of the head. I discovered, after some trial and error, that if I let the raw juice settle for three to four hours, the perfect amount of starch settled to the bottom of the pan. I could then pour the juice off, leaving the starch behind. The end result was rich, sweet, and tasted like nature's best sweet potato. I decided it would be great paired with duck.

This was the first step on a long journey. I discovered numerous other vegetables that can be made into rich, satisfying sauces. Some are lighter than others, and some take more time to make than others. All require a desire to experiment with the juicer, a degree of patience, and a mind open to new cooking techniques.

Along the way, I discarded my belief that fat was vital for flavor. Some writers and chefs insist that the flavor is in the fat, but if you taste a tablespoon of melted butter or chicken fat, you won't get a mouthful of flavor. You will get a mouthful of fat. Fat conducts flavor but it does not provide it. Without question, there is no replacement for cream and butter if you want resplendent creaminess, but there are other ways to make a good sauce.

With care and a desire for flavor, juice and pristine stock reductions result in sauces as delicious as any made with fat. I found that when you eliminate the fat, you also eliminate the ability to season the sauce with abandon. This makes it trickier to right an unbalanced sauce, but if you begin with the best and freshest vegetables and choose ingredients that love each other, chances are your sauce will naturally fall into balance. And the flavors will be refreshingly pure and simple.

BEING SLAVE TO THE SEASONS MEANS LIBERATION

I learned more about food in the four years I was chef at Heartbeat than in my entire career. Yet, in a very fundamental way, I relearned much of what I had always known from working side by side with my mother in her garden and sharing her appreciation for perfectly ripe produce. This gives me confidence as I now teach these principles to others.

When you rely on one vegetable for a sauce, seasonality takes on profound meaning. Even at the peak of my performance at Miche Mache, I never sliced into an onion or broke open a sweet potato to determine its freshness and judge its starch content. I pushed the seasons and relied on cooking techniques to manipulate food so that it tasted good. If a sweet potato was not perfect, a little brown sugar, nutmeg, and cinnamon fixed it up.

Now, I am a slave to the seasons, which has joyfully liberated me to look at food with a refreshed perspective. Nature designed our food supply in a marvelous way. In the early spring, foods green with freshness, like peas, asparagus, and young lettuces, spark our senses and chase away the winter's reliance on root vegetables. Spring quickly fades into summer with its explosive flavors that demand immediate consumption. Tree-ripened peaches must be consumed within a few days at the very latest, for example. With autumn come the heartier foods that hold up to long storage and preserving techniques perfected out of necessity through the generations.

Advances in technology have rendered many of these preserving techniques obsolete or quaint. I have nothing against technology—where would we be without refrigeration?— but some of these advances have allowed us to remove ourselves so far from the seasons and the land that we sacrifice flavor. Try eating a tomato from a supermarket in January. It tastes bland and mealy, because it was picked green, forced to ripen in a cold room filled with nitrogen gas, and then shipped far and wide. By the time the fruit turns red, it has been off the vine for weeks or months. No wonder it has no flavor!

If you have eaten tomatoes off the vine in high summer, you will never be satisfied with winter fruit. Instead, eat high-quality canned tomatoes in the wintertime. Yes, canned! Wait until you can get your hands on perfectly ripe summer tomatoes and enjoy their lusciousness, which needs no more embellishment than a sprinkling of salt and pepper.

I believe, because of methods such as those applied to tomatoes, that many vegetables and fruits have become secondary ingredients, rarely given much attention by cooks at home or in restaurants. But if you cook with the seasons, if you wait for the early spring's best asparagus and July's golden corn, you too will come to value nature's pure freshness.

I feel the same way about naturally raised poultry and meat. Try a chicken that is truly free-range: raised without being pumped full of antibiotics and growth enhancers and permitted to roam freely in a farmyard pecking for food. The meat is succulent and rich in flavor, and compared to factory-raised birds, there is very little fat.

Dedicated farmers across the country are trying to make a living growing organic fruits and vegetables and raising livestock naturally. The trick is finding them. Seek them out and talk to them at farmers' markets and roadside stands. Ask your local market to buy locally. Say you want fresh food—which means freshly picked, not unspoiled or frozen.

Everyone is seduced by convenience, and sometimes it seems the only way to go, but if you start caring more about taste and goodness and less about saving time, and if you support local farmers and merchants who carry responsibly raised foods, your dollars will be voting for the future of our environment and our food supply. And your taste buds will thank you.

So, get to the farm stand and taste food like you've never tasted it before. Take care of the planet while you take care of your family and yourself. And, yes, open this book and enjoy the recipes. It's a privilege to bring them to you.

appetizers and salads

summer melons with ginger 22

oven-roasted tomatoes with goat cheese
and extra-virgin olive oil 23

sautéed scallops with creamy corn sauce 24

tamari shrimp and scallops 27

sashimi of fluke with sweet shrimp 28

fresh oysters with ginger-sake mignonette 30

white bean dip 31

asian pear salad with tamari pecans
and maytag blue cheese 33

tamari pecans 34

roasted root vegetables and baby greens salad 35

heirloom tomato salad with aged
balsamic vinaigrette 37

fresh tuna and radish salad with wasabi dressing 38

My mother came from a family of melon farmers, and so she always had an abiding love for garden-grown melons, her favorites being cantaloupes and other muskmelons. I can remember seeing her standing in our backyard garden, coaxing the melons to ripen, as though her will alone could accelerate the process. When they were ripe and juicy, we cut them open, sprinkled the sweet flesh with ground ginger mixed with sugar, and then squeezed lime juice on them. Later, when I discovered fresh ginger, I looked for a way to use it instead of ground ginger and came up with this method. It's not overpowering, but the wisp of flavor from the ginger, mint, and lime is pure and mysterious.

I suggest putting the melons in the center of a picnic table with the ginger on a small tray nearby. Put the mint in a wineglass or small vase filled with water, and the lime wedges in a decorative bowl. Show your guests how to swipe the cut melons with ginger and then with mint before squeezing a little juice over all. Eat these wedges outside so there's no need for forks.

summer melons with ginger

SERVES 8 TO 10

Sturdy greens such as collards, chard, or escarole

1 ripe cantaloupe, halved, seeded, and cut into 16 wedges

1 ripe honeydew, gala, or other muskmelon, halved, seeded, and cut into 16 wedges

Two or three 1-inch pieces fresh ginger, halved horizontally

1 large bunch mint, with stems

2 to 4 limes, each cut into 8 wedges

Arrange the greens on a large tray or platter.

Place the melon wedges on the greens and serve.

Put the ginger, mint, and lime wedges near the melons. Each person should rub a piece of melon with the cut side of the ginger and then with a mint sprig, crushing it gently along the flesh of the melon. Squeeze a little lime juice on each melon wedge, and voilà!

I like to dry my own tomatoes; that way I can control the moisture content and have tomatoes that are moist, meaty, and syrupy with the concentrated flavor of sun-dried tomatoes. When their flavor is this intense, they stand up to goat cheese; fresh, raw tomatoes do better paired with mild cheeses such as mozzarella and young feta.

Peaches, figs, cherries, apricots, and nectarines can be dried using this method as long as they are ripe, moist, and full flavored to begin with.

oven-roasted tomatoes with goat cheese and extra-virgin olive oil

SERVES 6

2 tablespoons extra-virgin olive oil

1 tablespoon aged balsamic vinegar

6 vine-ripened tomatoes, such as Roma or any that are ripe and delicious, halved vertically

Salt and freshly ground pepper to taste

6 teaspoon-sized pieces fresh white goat cheese

6 sprigs rosemary

Preheat the oven to 200°F. If your oven does not have this temperature setting, set it on low.

In a large bowl, whisk 1 tablespoon of the oil with the vinegar. Add the halved tomatoes and toss very gently. Make sure each tomato is lightly coated with the dressing. Season with salt and pepper.

Arrange the tomatoes on a wire rack set on a baking sheet. Place the tomatoes, cut side up, on the rack and dry them in the oven for 4 to 6 hours. Turn the baking sheet frequently to promote even drying. The tomatoes will shrink considerably but will stay somewhat soft and syrupy. Do not let them dry completely (they should not resemble commercially produced chewy sun-dried tomatoes). Remove the tomatoes from the oven and let them cool on the rack.

Center a piece of cheese on each tomato. Fold the tomato slightly to cradle the cheese. Insert a rosemary sprig into one end of the tomato, through the cheese, and out the other end of the tomato to hold the tomato and cheese together. Repeat with the remaining tomatoes. Drizzle lightly with the remaining 1 tablespoon oil.

Let stand for 30 minutes before serving.

The beauty of corn juice, used to make this creamy sauce, is that it is self-thickening. No roux or processed starch is necessary for it to acquire its creamy silkiness. It does that all on its own as it's cooked. I pair it with scallops because they work so well together.

Among the useful skills Native Americans living along the Atlantic coast taught the New England settlers was to fertilize and aerate their fields with scallop and oyster shells and fish bones. These very same fields were used to grow native corn. It may sound romantic to wax on about this, but I believe this sustainable system of agriculture contributes to the natural affinity of some foods, like scallops and corn. If you've ever been to an authentic New England clam bake, you know that scallops—not lobsters—and fresh sweet corn are the stars!

sautéed scallops with creamy corn sauce

SERVES 4

8 sea scallops

Salt and freshly ground pepper to taste

2 teaspoons grapeseed oil

⅓ cup grilled corn kernels
(1 ear grilled corn, see page 158)

½ cup Creamy Corn Sauce (page 156)

Leaves from 1 small bunch epazote

1 tablespoon minced fresh chives

2 tablespoons huitlacoche sauce (page 165)

Fresh corn shoots, mâche, or pea shoots for garnish

Snipped fresh chives for garnish

Sprinkle each scallop with salt and pepper. Heat 1 teaspoon of the grapeseed oil in a nonstick sauté pan or skillet over medium-high heat. Add the scallops and sear for a minute or less, or until nicely browned on the bottom. Turn the scallops over, sear for about 30 seconds, and remove from the heat. Let the scallops sit in the hot pan off the heat so that they finish cooking gently.

In a small saucepan, heat the remaining 1 teaspoon grapeseed oil and add the corn kernels. Cook over low heat for about 2 minutes, or until they begin to release some moisture. Add the corn sauce and cook, stirring constantly, until just heated through. Be careful not to let the sauce simmer or it might curdle. Add the epazote and stir for a minute or so, or until you can taste the herb in the sauce. Stir in the chives and remove from the heat.

Spoon the sauce into the centers of 4 warmed plates. Drizzle a thin line of huitlacoche sauce around the edge of the corn sauce. Arrange 2 scallops in the center of the sauce on each plate and garnish with the greens and chives.

When my chef de cuisine at Heartbeat, John Mooney, created this dish, I was struck by its sensuousness. As it cooks, the scallop expands to meet the embrace of the shrimp in a miracle of geometry and reaction to heat. They have similar flavors but different textures, and for centuries both have teamed beautifully with Asian flavors. This easy recipe is testament to such affinity.

tamari shrimp and scallops

SERVES 4

8 sea scallops

8 large shrimp, shelled and deveined

1 cup tamari sauce

Freshly ground pepper to taste

4 teaspoons canola oil

GARNISH

4 fresh green shiso leaves

4 fresh red shiso leaves

Nestle a scallop in the curve of each shrimp. Use 2 short bamboo skewers to secure the shrimp to the scallop. Set aside.

Pour the tamari into a metal bowl set over a small saucepan with about 2 inches of simmering water. Cook over medium-high heat for 30 to 40 minutes, or until reduced by half and slightly thickened. A salt crust will form on top of the reducing tamari. Do not stir the crust into the tamari. Instead, carefully pour the tamari from the pan, leaving the salt crust behind. This will keep the tamari from being too salty.

Heat a medium sauté pan or skillet over medium heat until hot. Season each seafood skewer lightly with pepper and then brush lightly first with the canola oil and then with the tamari reduction.

Sear the skewers for about 2 minutes on each side, or until lightly browned. To serve, spoon a little tamari into the center of each of 4 plates. Place 2 of the skewers on the sauce and garnish with the shiso leaves. Do not use too much of the tamari reduction; it's very salty.

Other than foraged foods, ocean-caught wild fish are the only truly natural, organic food available in our changing world. Most super-fresh ocean fish can be eaten raw, which I think is the best representation of their flavor. When I moved to the East Coast, I discovered fluke and it quickly became one of my favorites. Fish love the sharpness of citrus, which is why I serve this with a sauce spiked with fresh lime juice. I always try to make this with the small, sweet shrimp called *ama ebi*. These tiny cold-water shrimp, best eaten raw, melt in your mouth with amazing sweetness—hence their nickname, "sweet shrimp." You can find them in Japanese markets, usually frozen.

I fondly recall a drift-boat fishing trip with friends. I boarded the boat wearing a tool belt equipped with sharp knives, a canister of sea salt, and squeeze bottles filled with lemon juice, soy sauce, and wasabi. My fellow passengers thought I was nuts—until I started slicing and seasoning the various fish we caught! Did I mention that I had some chilled sake, too?

sashimi of fluke with sweet shrimp

SERVES **4**

16 very thin slices sashimi-grade fluke, each about 2½ inches long and 1 inch wide

32 sprigs cilantro

Thirty-two 1½-inch-long pieces fresh chives

24 small (30 count) sweet shrimp or regular shrimp, shelled, deveined, cooked, and chilled

2 tablespoons plus 2 teaspoons fish sauce (nam pla)

2 tablespoons plus 2 teaspoons fresh lime juice

Sambal olek or red Thai or Vietnamese chili sauce to taste

Lay the slices of fish on a work surface. Lay 2 cilantro sprigs and 2 chive pieces on each slice and roll so that the tops of the herbs extend from one end.

Stand the rolls on end on a chilled plate and arrange the shrimp along with them.

Combine the fish sauce and lime juice in a small ramekin or sauce dish. Stir in chili sauce to make the sauce as spicy as you like.

As everyone knows, oysters must be impeccably fresh—they should smell only of the sea, not of mud. Muddy shells can indicate a recent harvest, but if the oysters tucked inside those shells smell muddy after they have been washed, stay away from them. East Coast oysters are creamy and mildly briny; West Coast oysters are crisper and have great mineral properties. Either way, nothing beats plump fresh oysters, served over ice and very cold. The only accompaniment they need, if any, is something bright and snappy, like this citrusy ginger relish.

fresh oysters with
ginger-sake mignonette

SERVES 6

24 raw oysters, shucked and nestled in the deep half shell

1½ tablespoons minced fresh ginger

1 tablespoon minced shallots

1 tablespoon minced red bell pepper

1½ tablespoons fresh lime juice

1 tablespoon chilled sake

6 small lemon wedges

6 small lime wedges

6 sprigs chervil or flat-leaf parsley

Fill 6 rimmed shallow soup bowls with crushed ice. Arrange 4 oyster shells on the ice around the perimeter of each bowl.

In a small bowl, stir the ginger, shallots, bell pepper, lime juice, and sake together. Divide among 6 ramekins or small, pretty bowls and set in the center of the ice in each bowl. Garnish with the lemon and lime wedges and sprigs of chervil or parsley.

Once you decide not to serve butter, as we did when I opened Heartbeat, you face the challenge of how to serve bread without it. Oil is an obvious alternative, but bread soaks up so much oil, I didn't think it would be fair to customers watching their fat intake. When I started thinking about some sort of dip, I remembered dunking chunks of crusty country bread in a wonderful white bean soup. I modified the recipe so that it became more of a dip than a soup, with an intensified garlicky flavor tamed by the fresh rosemary. It adds some carbs to a meal, but it also substitutes for the lushness of butter and oil. If 8 cups is too much for your purposes, halve the recipe. But remember—it keeps well!

white bean dip

MAKES ABOUT **8** CUPS

2 cups (1 pound) dried white beans

8 garlic cloves, peeled

2 bunches rosemary

Salt and freshly ground pepper to taste

Chunks of crusty bread for serving

Rinse and pick over the beans. Soak in water to cover by 2 inches for at least 6 hours, or up to 24 hours. Drain.

Put the garlic cloves in a small saucepan and add cold water to cover. Bring to a full simmer over medium-high heat and then immediately drain. Return the garlic cloves to the saucepan. Cover with more cold water and repeat. Do this a total of 5 times. Set the blanched garlic cloves aside.

Put the beans in a stockpot or large saucepan and add water to cover by 2 inches. Bring to a rapid simmer. Skim any foam that rises to the surface. Reduce the heat to low and simmer for about 1½ hours, or until the beans are tender but not mushy.

Drain the beans in a colander set over a bowl. Reserve the cooking liquid. Transfer the beans to a blender or a food processor. Add the garlic cloves and puree until smooth, adding as much of the cooking liquid as necessary for a thick, spreadable or dippable consistency.

Gently stir the bean dip with the rosemary bunches for about 3 minutes, or until the dip is fragrant with the scent of rosemary. Discard the rosemary. Season with salt and pepper and serve warm with the bread. Or, transfer to a lidded container, cover, and refrigerate for up to 1 week. Bring to a simmer over low heat before serving.

Ever since American chefs discovered the amazing food marriage of tree fruits and blue cheese, they have served the two in many forms. Pears are classic, but nearly all tree fruits work well. Go through the seasons: cherries, peaches, plums, apples, and then pears. As much as I like them all, pears remain my favorite. For this salad, I like crisp, moist Asian pears (also called Japanese pears), which can be sliced ahead of time because they don't brown easily. They also are fairly easy to find.

The blue cheese clearly is the dominant ingredient. You don't usually think of cheese with Asian flavors, but in this preparation, it's dynamite. Everything works here: The tamari takes the pecans to a new taste level, and the bitter greens and the reduced pear juice dressing provide just the right spark for this rich, sweet, and salty salad.

asian pear salad with tamari pecans and maytag blue cheese

SERVES 4

2 tablespoons pear or cider vinegar

4 teaspoons Pear Syrup (page 158)

1 teaspoon Extra-Virgin O Lemon Oil or unflavored extra-virgin olive oil

6 cups mixed bitter salad greens, such as baby mustard, lovage, arugula, dandelion, and mizuna

¼ cup chopped Tamari Pecans (page 34)

¼ cup dried currants or chopped raisins

¼ cup crumbled chilled blue cheese, such as Maytag

Salt and freshly ground pepper to taste

1 ripe Asian pear, cored, peeled, and thinly sliced

In a small salad bowl, combine the vinegar and syrup. Whisk in the oil and set aside.

In a large bowl, combine the greens, pecans, and currants. Sprinkle with the cheese and season lightly with salt and pepper. Whisk the dressing again and drizzle it over the salad.

Toss the salad gently and briefly; you do not want the cheese to crumble any further and clump together.

Divide the salad among 4 chilled salad plates. Fan the pear slices over each serving.

tamari pecans

1 tablespoon tamari sauce

2 teaspoons molasses

Cayenne pepper and salt to taste

1 cup pecan halves

Preheat the oven to 350°F.

In a shallow bowl, stir the tamari and molasses together to blend. Season with cayenne and salt.

Add the pecans and toss until they are coated. Transfer the pecans to a clean kitchen towel and let drain briefly.

Spread the pecans on a wire rack set on a baking sheet and roast for about 10 minutes, or until fairly dry and toasted.

Remove from the oven and let cool completely on the rack. Chop the pecans into ¼-inch pieces.

What I particularly like about this salad is that the flavors change as you eat it: The greens mingle with the beet syrup and the salad just tastes richer. I have dubbed this the "metamorphosis salad." It celebrates the good root vegetables available in the fall, which taste full and sweet when you roast them (for instructions on how to roast these and other vegetables, see page 166). You can use different vegetables and greens and alter your choice of vegetable syrup as you get more confident making these sweet syrups. For example, you could try rutabaga syrup or golden beet syrup. One more note: Make sure you err on the side of large baby carrots and don't use the tiny ones, which don't have as much flavor when roasted.

roasted root vegetables and baby greens salad

SERVES 4

4 baby red beets, roasted and halved

4 baby golden beets, roasted and halved

4 cipollini or pearl onions, roasted

4 large baby carrots, roasted and halved lengthwise

4 red radishes, roasted and halved

2 tablespoons Red Beet Syrup (page 157)

2 tablespoons extra-virgin olive oil

2 tablespoons aged balsamic vinegar

Salt and freshly ground pepper to taste

8 cups mixed baby salad greens

Arrange the vegetables so that they circle the centers of 4 chilled salad plates. Drizzle the syrup on the plate just inside the vegetable circles.

In a large bowl, whisk the oil and vinegar together and season with salt and pepper.

Add the salad greens and toss to mix. Divide the salad among the plates, piling them in the center of each plate. Serve immediately.

If you ever had an aunt, uncle, grandparent, or neighbor who grew his or her own "home-grown" tomatoes and you recall them as the best you ever tasted, you have probably tasted an heirloom tomato. These often irregularly shaped, colorful tomatoes are grown from seeds that have been passed down through generations of small farmers and backyard gardeners. If you've never tasted them, they are worth seeking out at farmers' markets, roadside stands, or from a neighbor's backyard. Use any combination that you can find if you can't find the ones listed below. If you grow tomatoes, get hold of some heirloom seeds and harvest your own. Of course, if you can't find them, use the best local farm tomatoes you can buy—but make sure they are perfectly ripe and fragrant.

Nothing is more humbling than a good tomato. It needs no more embellishment than salt and pepper, so when you add extra ingredients, they should be of the highest quality. This salad relies on the gentle use of excellent oil and vinegar and super-fresh herbs.

heirloom tomato salad with aged balsamic vinaigrette

SERVES 4 TO 6

2 small Brandywine tomatoes

1 Purple Cherokee tomato

1 Big Daddy Sunshine tomato

1 Watermelon tomato

5 Green Zebra tomatoes

¼ cup loosely packed shredded fresh basil leaves, plus basil sprigs for garnish

2 tablespoons minced fresh chives

¼ cup aged balsamic vinegar

2 tablespoons Extra-Virgin O Lemon Oil or unflavored extra-virgin olive oil

Salt and freshly cracked pepper to taste

Cut the tomatoes into different shapes but of a similar thickness: Slice, quarter, or cube them.

In a large bowl, combine the tomatoes, shredded basil, chives, vinegar, and oil. Toss gently. Season with salt and pepper. Serve right away, garnished with basil sprigs.

Raw tuna is beautiful: silky smooth, with a rich mouth feel that is reminiscent of a well-made pâté. When something is so good, there's no reason to cook it. In this way, tuna could be called the "tomato of the fish world": When it's fresh and perfect, why tamper with it? It's excellent on its own with just a little coarse sea salt. This dish is a celebration of raw flavors and textures: crisp radishes and sprouts, the lively surprise of mint, and the warmth of cilantro. Served with the wasabi dressing, it's perfect as a cold hors d'oeuvre or as a first course.

fresh tuna and radish salad with wasabi dressing

SERVES **4**

WASABI DRESSING

3 tablespoons wasabi powder

3 tablespoons silken tofu

1 tablespoon rice vinegar

1 tablespoon yuzu juice or fresh lemon juice

1 tablespoon mirin

TUNA AND RADISH SALAD

4 ounces assorted radishes, sliced paper thin or shredded (about 1 cup)

2 tablespoons fresh mint leaves

2 tablespoons fresh cilantro leaves

2 tablespoons daikon sprouts or other peppery sprouts

1½ tablespoons yuzu juice or fresh lemon juice

1½ tablespoons mirin

1 pound sushi-grade tuna, preferably yellowfin, cut into 16 slices about ¼ inch thick

Coarse sea salt for sprinkling

TO MAKE THE DRESSING: In a small bowl, combine all the ingredients and whisk until smooth.

TO MAKE THE SALAD: In a large bowl, combine the radishes, mint, cilantro, and sprouts. Add the yuzu or lemon juice and mirin and toss to mix well. Divide among 4 chilled plates.

Arrange 4 slices of tuna over each mound of salad, overlapping the slices slightly.

Drizzle about 1 tablespoon of the dressing around the salad on each plate. Finish by sprinkling sea salt over the tuna slices. Store leftover dressing in the refrigerator in a tightly covered container for up to 1 week.

2

soups

sweet corn and vegetable chowder 42

heirloom tomato soup 45

green tomato soup with heirloom tomatoes
and vidalia onion garnish 47

heirloom squash soup with roasted chestnuts 48

black-eyed pea soup with wilted greens 49

basmati and black rice juk 51

pan-toasted garlic and wilted spinach soup 52

celery root and truffle soup 53

This recipe proves a belief of mine. When you cook with ingredients that sound good in your head, they will taste good, too. I feel this way about vanilla and corn, which may seem like a strange pair, but once you try this combination, you'll like it. My mom's creamed corn was the best, and she always added vanilla extract to it, which pushed it over the edge into the realm of legendary. The first time I saw an actual vanilla bean, I was amazed, having until then thought of vanilla only as an extract. I mailed some beans to my mother, who was equally amazed. I quickly fell in love with their rich flavor, and started to think of foods to pair it with, such as rutabagas, beets, and shellfish. But I also remembered my mother's creamed corn and so tried vanilla in this chowder. Most people can't believe there is no cream in this soup, but it's the corn juice—which thickens naturally because of its own starch—that gives the chowder its rich, satisfying texture. The vanilla bean boosts its fullness and richness.

sweet corn and vegetable chowder

SERVES **4**

About 24 fresh ears corn, shucked

1 Yukon Gold potato

½ split vanilla bean, or
¼ teaspoon pure vanilla extract

2 pounds fresh or frozen edamame, fava, or lima beans (about 1 cup shelled)

1 to 2 tablespoons water

Salt and freshly ground pepper to taste

½ cup shredded spinach, sorrel, or arugula

1 tablespoon julienned lemon zest

1 tablespoon fresh lemon juice

CONTINUED

Preheat the oven to 450°F. Place 2 ears of corn directly on the oven rack and roast, turning occasionally, until golden brown, 20 to 25 minutes. Remove from the oven and let cool. When cool, cut the roasted corn kernels off the cob. You should have about 1½ cups.

Meanwhile, cook the potato in salted boiling water until tender in the center when pierced, 20 to 25 minutes. Drain and let cool to the touch. Slip off the skin and cut the potato into ¼-inch dice.

With a large, sharp knife, cut the kernels off the remaining ears of corn. Run the kernels through a vegetable juicer. You should have about 4 cups of juice. Combine the corn juice and the vanilla bean in a medium nonreactive saucepan. Bring to a simmer over medium-low heat, stirring constantly so the liquid doesn't curdle. The natural starch in the juice will thicken it to a sauce consistency. The degree of thickness will depend on the amount of starch in the corn. If the soup is too thick, thin it with a little water or lemon juice. Remove from the heat.

sweet corn and vegetable chowder

CONTINUED

Fish out the vanilla bean and, with the tip of a small knife, scrape the seeds from the bean into the soup; discard the pod. If the soup appears a little broken, don't worry. Blend the soup in a blender at medium speed for a silky-smooth consistency. Return the soup to the pot.

Put the roasted corn kernels, beans, and potato in a medium sauté pan or skillet with the water. Bring to a simmer over a medium heat and season with salt and pepper. Simmer for a few minutes until the vegetables are hot. Pour off the water and add the vegetables to the soup. Stir in the shredded spinach or other greens, the lemon zest, lemon juice, salt, and pepper.

NOTE: IF THE CORN MILK CURDLES DURING COOKING, DON'T WORRY. BEAT THE CURDLED MILK WITH AN ELECTRIC MIXER SET ON MEDIUM SPEED UNTIL IT RETURNS TO ITS PERFECT SMOOTHNESS BEFORE YOU ADD THE REST OF THE VEGETABLES.

When something is as good as ripe summer tomatoes, you almost can't get enough of them, so I try to come up with as many ways to prepare them as I can. I can still remember waiting for the tomatoes in my mom's garden to ripen. She wouldn't let us eat any that had not fallen off the vine, and I used to "accidentally" poke or prod an almost-ripe fruit with the hoe or spade, hoping it would fall off. If Mom caught me, I was in trouble! She made a soup similar to this and kept it in the refrigerator for us to eat at any time of day. I remember drinking it for breakfast instead of orange juice.

Making soup is a natural way to get pure tomato flavor; you can even use slightly over-ripe tomatoes. I like to use red and yellow tomatoes for the sheer beauty of them. Different types of tomatoes have different levels of acidity, so I include honey in the recipe list to use if you need it.

heirloom tomato soup

SERVES 6

2 pounds very ripe red heirloom tomatoes, such as Brandywine or Purple Cherokee, or any good, ripe red tomato

¼ cup packed torn fresh basil leaves, plus 6 sprigs basil for garnish

2 pounds very ripe yellow heirloom tomatoes, such as Lemon Boy or Big Daddy Sunshine, or any good, ripe yellow tomato

¼ cup extra-virgin olive oil

1 tablespoon honey, if needed

Salt and freshly ground pepper to taste

Cut the red tomatoes into wedges large enough to fit through the food tube of the juicer. Put half of the torn basil leaves in the juicer's tube, followed by the red tomatoes. Juice these together. Set the red juice aside.

Cut the yellow tomatoes into wedges large enough to fit through the food tube of the juicer. Put the remaining torn basil leaves in the juicer's tube, followed by the yellow tomatoes. Juice these together. Set the yellow juice aside.

Put the yellow tomato juice in a large blender. (Because both juices are blended in the same blender, start with the yellow tomato juice to keep the red juice from coloring the yellow.) Add half the olive oil, half the honey, if needed, and salt and pepper. Blend. Pour the yellow tomato juice into a pitcher or large spouted measuring cup.

Repeat with the red tomato juice, the remaining oil, the remaining honey, if needed, and more salt and pepper.

Pour the 2 juices simultaneously into the center of each of 6 chilled bowls. They will make a pretty pattern. Garnish each bowl with a basil sprig.

Despite what most people think, not all green tomatoes are unripe. Fully ripe green tomato varieties, such as Evergreen and Zebra, share all the luxuriousness of their red and yellow cousins. I like them because they are lighter flavored, a little more acidic, and don't taste quite as much of minerals but are naturally sweet. I find that chilled tomato soup made with green tomatoes is especially refreshing—and seeking them out is a journey worth taking.

green tomato soup with heirloom tomatoes and vidalia onion garnish

SERVES 4

6 Green Zebra tomatoes, each about 3 inches in diameter, ripened to the point of blushing yellow and beginning to soften

¼ cup packed fresh basil leaves, plus 4 to 6 large basil leaves, julienned, for garnish

2 pints green grape tomatoes, stemmed

2 tablespoons Extra-Virgin O Lemon Oil or unflavored extra-virgin olive oil

Salt and freshly ground pepper to taste

4 heirloom or regular cherry tomatoes, chilled and halved lengthwise

4 baby pear tomatoes, chilled and halved lengthwise

½ small Vidalia onion, thinly sliced

2 tablespoons aged balsamic vinegar, preferably 8 years old

Choose the 4 most nicely shaped Zebra tomatoes. These will be used to serve the soup. Set them upright on the counter, stem side up, and cut the top ½ inch off each one. Reserve the tomato caps. With a paring knife or soup spoon, carefully scoop out the pulp, leaving a wall thick enough to hold the tomato together. Use your finger or the spoon handle to remove the seeds from the inside of the tomatoes and the tomato caps. Reserve the tomato pulp and seeds.

Stem and quarter the remaining Zebra tomatoes.

Turn on the vegetable juicer and insert the packed fresh basil leaves into the feeding shoot. Follow these with the quartered Zebra tomatoes, the grape tomatoes, and the reserved tomato pulp and seeds.

Transfer the solids from the juicer's catch container to a fine-mesh sieve. Press the solids through the strainer into the tomato juice, using the back of a large spoon. Pour the juice into a blender and add 1 tablespoon of the oil. Blend on medium speed for 20 to 30 seconds, or until smooth and blended. Season with salt and pepper.

To serve, place a hollowed-out tomato in the center of each plate. Pour the soup into each tomato and then replace the reserved cap. Arrange the cherry and pear tomatoes around the hollowed-out tomatoes, cut sides up. Sprinkle the Vidalia onion over the tomatoes and garnish with the julienned basil leaves. Season with salt and pepper, then drizzle with balsamic vinegar and the remaining 1 tablespoon oil.

Kabocha is my favorite autumn squash. It looks similar to acorn squash but has a deeper, sweeter flavor and meatier texture. Squash are similar to each other, and so you can't go wrong using butternut, Hubbard, Delicata, or acorn in place of kabocha. There will be slight differences in taste, but very subtle ones. I often like to mix squashes when I make this soup, with roasted chestnuts added for richness and texture.

heirloom squash soup with roasted chestnuts

SERVES 6

3 pounds kabocha or other winter squash, peeled, seeded, and cut into 1-inch cubes

2 tablespoons olive oil

Salt and freshly ground pepper to taste

1 Vidalia onion or other sweet, mild onion, cut into ½-inch-thick slices

2 teaspoons grapeseed oil

6 Roasted Garlic Cloves (page 159)

2 cinnamon sticks

3 green cardamom pods

½ small red Thai chili, finely sliced

4 cups Roasted Vegetable Stock (page 163)

¼ cup plain low-fat yogurt, drained (see below)

2 tablespoons packed shredded fresh tarragon leaves

12 chestnuts, roasted, peeled, and sliced (page 83)

Preheat the oven to 350°F.

In a large bowl, combine the squash cubes, olive oil, salt, and pepper. Toss to coat. Spread the squash on a baking sheet and roast for 30 to 40 minutes, or until tender. Transfer to a large saucepan.

Coat the onion slices with grapeseed oil and season with salt and pepper. Spread on a baking sheet and roast for 10 to 12 minutes, or until the bottoms are browned. Turn the slices over and roast for about 10 minutes longer.

Add the onion, roasted garlic, cinnamon, cardamom pods, and chilies to the squash. Add the stock and bring to a simmer over medium-high heat. Reduce the heat to medium-low and cook for 20 to 30 minutes, or until the squash begins to dissolve.

Remove the cinnamon sticks and cardamom pods and discard. Transfer the soup to a blender or food processor and purée until smooth. Season with salt and pepper to taste.

Put the drained yogurt in a small bowl and stir in the tarragon until well blended.

Pour the soup into 6 warmed soup bowls. Garnish with the yogurt and chestnuts.

DRAINING YOGURT: Spoon plain yogurt into a sieve lined with a double thickness of cheesecloth or a coffee filter and set over a bowl. Refrigerate for at least 1 hour or up to 8 hours.

The easiest way to make this soup is with leftover black-eyed peas and stewed greens. Because my mom was an excellent Southern cook, these ingredients were often handy when I was growing up. I loved digging with a ladle to the bottom of the pea pot for mashed peas, which I put in a saucepan. Next, I skimmed some liquid off the top of the pot, added it to pan, and then tossed in a handful of leftover greens. Great soup! Since you may not be fortunate enough to have my mom cook in your kitchen, I've devised a soup with the same comfort level but the added benefit of fresh greens.

black-eyed pea soup with wilted greens

SERVES 6

½ pound black-eyed peas, rinsed, soaked in cold water to cover for 2 hours, and drained

4 cups Ham Hock Stock (page 162)

1 small onion, chopped

2 tablespoons molasses

Salt and freshly ground pepper to taste

1 pound mixed bitter greens, such as mustard, arugula, and kale

In a large saucepan, combine the peas, stock, and onion. Bring to a simmer over medium-high heat. Reduce the heat to medium-low and cook, uncovered, for 20 to 25 minutes, or until the peas are tender but not mushy.

Use a large ladle to remove about half the peas. Set these aside.

Cook the remaining peas over medium-low heat until they begin to break apart. Whisk the soup vigorously until the peas break down and create a lightly thickened soup.

Return the reserved peas to the soup. Add the molasses, salt, and pepper. Return to a simmer and add the greens. Gently stir the greens until they just begin to wilt. Taste and adjust the seasoning. Serve immediately.

I was attracted to this soup as a way to make a creamy soup without cream. Plus, it's a good way to get more rice into the diet. Juk (also called jook and congee), as it is made in Southeast Asia, is a chunky, everyday soup, and you can make yours that way by omitting the straining process. I like to strain it for a more elegant soup, not unlike vichysoisse, with the comforting nuttiness of rice. For full flavor, I use chicken stock, but for a vegetarian version, I use water. You can also experiment with different kinds of rice. Cooking times will vary depending on the rice. Here, I use sweet-tasting, earthy Thai black rice, which needs longer cooking than white rice. Sometimes called sweet black rice, it's available in Asian markets, specialty stores, and many supermarkets. In Thailand, as here, it's very often mixed with while rice.

basmati and black rice juk

SERVES 6

1 cup Thai black rice

8 quarts Rich Chicken Stock (page 160) or water

¾ cup basmati rice

4 to 6 Roasted Garlic Cloves (page 159)

2 tablespoons freshly grated horseradish

Salt and freshly ground pepper to taste

In a large saucepan, combine the black rice and half of the stock or water. Bring to a simmer over medium-high heat, stirring constantly. Adjust the heat to medium-low and cover to maintain constant simmer for 1½ to 2 hours, or until the rice can be easily smashed between two fingers. You may need to add additional stock or water if the lid to the pot does not fit tightly.

Using another large saucepan, cook the basmati rice the same way. The basmati will need to cook 1½ to 2 hours.

Add half the roasted garlic cloves and half the horseradish to each pan and simmer for 5 minutes. Pass both broths separately through a fine-mesh sieve into different containers for pouring. If you like a chunkier soup, use a food mill fitted with a fine or medium blade, which is less tedious than using a sieve.

Pour the liquids simultaneously into soup bowls so that each is half-filled with each one. Season with salt and pepper and serve immediately.

No flavor is purer than that of water. Oh boy, you're saying about now: This guy is whacked! But think about it. The flavor of water is so pristinely clean it allows other flavors to shine through. Try to munch on some roasted chicken bones and see how they taste. Now, simmer these same bones in water and taste the resulting broth. Delicious. This may be a simple culinary revelation but is worth thinking about.

For instance, who would have thought that garlic, spinach, and water could constitute a complete recipe—but they do. Garlic and spinach are happy together, as anyone who has eaten spinach wilted with garlic knows. If you just add water, you have an amazing soup. To make this more substantial and reminiscent of the soups of the Mediterranean, add some cooked pasta and freshly grated pecorino cheese.

pan-toasted garlic and wilted spinach soup

SERVES 6

¼ cup extra-virgin olive oil

16 cloves garlic, thinly sliced

1 pound fresh spinach, stemmed and chopped

Salt to taste

5 cups water or Rich Chicken Stock (page 160)

Freshly ground pepper to taste

½ lemon, or more to taste

In a large, heavy soup pot, combine the olive oil and garlic cloves. Set the pot over medium heat and cook, stirring, for about 5 minutes, or until the garlic turns light brown.

Increase the heat to high and immediately add the spinach. Sprinkle the spinach with salt to encourage it to give up its moisture. Cook, stirring occasionally, until it wilts completely and most of the moisture evaporates.

Pour the water into the pot and bring to a simmer. Simmer for 1 minute, then season with salt and pepper to taste. Don't be afraid to be generous with the seasoning. Squeeze the lemon into the soup. Ladle into bowls and serve immediately.

No doubt about it, celery root is an underestimated vegetable. Sure, it's big and ugly with lots of knobs and looks like something that could never taste delicious, but nothing could be further from the truth. And you don't have to try hard to make it truly wonderful. When simmered gently, it is pureed into as silken a soup as has ever graced a spoon. That celery root and truffles taste good together is no secret. You need almost nothing else, which explains the limited ingredient list for this soup.

celery root and truffle soup

SERVES 6

1 to 1½ pounds celery root, peeled and diced (about 6 cups)

6 cups Rich Chicken Stock (page 160), or more as needed

¼ cup extra-virgin olive oil

2 tablespoons truffle oil

Salt and freshly ground pepper to taste

1 to 1½ ounces black truffle, thinly sliced

In a large saucepan, combine the celery root, stock, and olive oil. Bring to a simmer over medium heat. Reduce the heat so that the liquid is barely simmering. Cover and cook for 30 to 45 minutes, or until the celery root is very tender. Strain through a fine-mesh sieve, pressing gently with the back of a large spoon to extract as much liquid as possible. Reserve the liquid.

Transfer the celery root to a blender or food processor and purée until very smooth.

Add cooking liquid as needed to achieve the consistency of a smooth soup. You will probably need all of it. If you use a blender, you may have to do this in batches.

Transfer the soup to a pot or bowl. Stir in the truffle oil, then season with salt and pepper. Divide the soup among 6 warmed soup bowls. Place 2 truffle slices in the center of each bowl. Julienne the remaining slices and sprinkle over the soup.

fish and shellfish 3

spicy grilled snapper with
ginger and lemongrass 56

roasted monkfish with porcini mushrooms
and fava beans 59

sautéed halibut with celery root and truffle 61

miso salmon with english pea sauce 62

cured salmon with caramelized cauliflower 64

pan-roasted cod with celery and heirloom potatoes 67

steamed black bass with kombu noodles
and mushroom dashi 69

crab cakes with papaya and jicama salad 70

grilled prawns with fennel and onions 71

Corn is best when grilled in its husk, chicken and ribs on the bone, and root vegetables in their jackets. Likewise, fish is best grilled with its skin and on the bone. This provides protection from the heat of the grill and intensifies the flavor of the fish. Nevertheless, grilling fish is always challenging. It falls apart easily, and the skin and flesh stick to the grill. The flesh also flakes and separates, and the fish easily divides into small, unattractive pieces.

I have addressed this by using the same flavoring ingredients used to marinate the fish as "flavor mats" on which to cook the fish. I begin by laying the fish on one of these mats and then halfway through grilling, I roll the fish onto the second mat. The mats provide an interesting, extra-smoky flavor even as they keep the fish from sticking. Another advantage to this recipe is that the fish can be prepared a day in advance up to the point of grilling.

spicy grilled snapper
with ginger and lemongrass

SERVES 4

SAMBAL BARBECUE SAUCE

1 cup oyster sauce

1 cup mirin

2/3 cup rice vinegar

2 stalks lemongrass (white part only), peeled and thinly sliced

1/4 cup thinly sliced peeled fresh ginger

2 star anise pods

1 tablespoon sambal olek or red Thai or Vietnamese chili sauce

CONTINUED

In a medium saucepan, combine all the ingredients for the barbecue sauce. Bring to a simmer over medium heat and cook for 15 to 20 minutes, or until the sauce tastes full and mellow.

Strain through a fine-mesh sieve and let cool. Reserve the solids to stuff into the cavity of the fish.

To grill the snapper, score the skin of the fish with a sharp knife to prevent curling during cooking. Do so by making a shallow incision on the diagonal from the dorsal fin to the belly. Next, make 4 to 6 incisions from the head to the tail.

Stuff the cavities of the fish with the reserved solids from the sauce. Rub about 1 tablespoon of the cooled sauce over each side of the fish.

Lay 3 stalks of the lightly smashed lemongrass across the bottom of a casserole or baking pan just large enough to hold both fish without stacking. Scatter half the ginger, limes, onion slices, and lemon verbena over the bottom of the casserole. This will provide a flavor base for the fish to rest on while marinating.

spicy grilled snapper
with ginger and lemongrass

CONTINUED

GRILLED SNAPPER

2 yellowtail snappers or red snappers,
cleaned and scaled

7 stalks lemongrass (white part only),
peeled, 6 stalks lightly smashed
with a mallet and 1 stalk thinly sliced

½ cup thinly sliced peeled fresh ginger

2 limes, thinly sliced

1 yellow onion, thinly sliced

10 sprigs lemon verbena (optional)

Lay the fish in the casserole and pour half of the remaining sauce over them. You should have about 1 cup sauce left. Arrange the remaining 3 smashed lemongrass stalks, the ginger, lime, onion, and lemon verbena on top of the fish. Cover tightly and refrigerate for 8 hours or overnight.

Prepare a fire in a charcoal grill or preheat a gas grill to medium hot.

Remove the layer of herbs and lay them on a medium-hot part of the grill, avoiding the hottest sections. Lay the fish side by side on top of the herbs. This will provide flavor and prevent sticking.

Grill the fish for 6 to 8 minutes. Baste each with about 2 tablespoons of the remaining sauce. Arrange the herbs from the bottom of the casserole next to the fish on the grill. Use a large spatula to roll the fish onto these herbs, exposing the uncooked sides to the heat of the grill. The rolling method will keep the tender fish from falling apart. Sprinkle the thinly sliced lemongrass on top of the fish. Cook the fish 4 to 6 minutes longer, basting with the remaining sauce. Place a baking sheet next to the fish and roll the fish onto it with the spatula. Serve immediately.

I love this fish because it's so damned versatile. It has been dubbed the "meat of fish" and is also called the "poor man's lobster," but for me a more apt term for this workhorse is the "smart man's steak." Monkfish can be roasted, seared, poached, and grilled, and once it's cooked, it can be sliced, just like meat. Monk, as it's affectionately known, has dense, moist, flavorful meat that stands up here to the richness of the garlicky broth, the earthiness of the porcini, and the heft of the fava beans. I don't know any other fish that could do this. This potent dish boasts a land-sea balance few others do, which is one reason I love it. If you're really hungry but want to eat fish, this is the ticket.

roasted monkfish with porcini mushrooms and fava beans

SERVES 6

Six 8-ounce monkfish loins

Salt and freshly ground pepper to taste

2 tablespoons grapeseed oil

6 large porcini mushrooms, cleaned and cut into ¼-inch-thick slices

1 pound fava beans, shelled, blanched, and peeled (see page 158), or 2 cups lima beans

3 cups Roasted Garlic Stock (page 159)

¼ cup torn fresh flat-leaf parsley leaves

Preheat the oven to 400°F.

Season each monkfish loin with salt and pepper.

Heat a large ovenproof skillet over high heat. Add the oil and cook the monkfish for 6 to 8 minutes, turning once or twice, or until nicely browned on all sides. Transfer the skillet to the oven and roast the fish for 3 minutes, or until opaque throughout.

Put the fish on a warmed platter, cover loosely, and set aside while you finish the dish.

Add the porcini mushrooms to the skillet and cook for about 5 minutes, or until softened and browned. Add the beans and stock and simmer for about 2 minutes, or until heated through. Season with salt and pepper to taste.

Cut each monkfish loin into 3 medallions, or rounds. Stand 3 medallions in the center of each of 6 warmed bowls. Divide the porcini broth among the bowls. Sprinkle liberally with parsley and season with salt and pepper to taste. Serve immediately.

Halibut loves celery root and celery root loves truffles. Put all three together and you'll discover how good this combination is! It's love by association. Halibut is a mild, subtly flavored fish. Both celery root and truffles are mild, too. When you taste this dish, you have to slow down and consider what your taste buds are experiencing: soft, warm flavors with long, lingering finishes. One word of caution: All the ingredients must be of the highest quality. Even the slightest compromise will diminish the meal.

sautéed halibut with celery root and truffle

SERVES 6

2½ pounds celery root, peeled and cut into ½-inch cubes

About 3 cups Rich Fish Stock (page 162) or Rich Chicken Stock (page 160)

Six 6-ounce skinless halibut fillets

2 tablespoons grapeseed oil

Salt and freshly ground pepper to taste

3 cups loosely packed baby pea shoots (dau miu)

1 cup julienned celery (about ¾ inch long)

2 ounces truffle, shaved and julienned (see Note)

1 tablespoon sherry vinegar

3 tablespoons truffle oil

Put the celery root in a medium saucepan and add just enough stock to cover. Bring to a low boil over medium heat, reduce the heat, and simmer gently for about 40 minutes, or until the celery root is soft enough to purée. Drain and reserve the cooking liquid.

Transfer the celery root to a blender or food processor and process until smooth. Add enough of the reserved cooking liquid to process until the celery puree is the consistency of soft polenta. Set aside and cover to keep warm.

Heat a large nonstick skillet over medium-high heat. While it's heating, rub the fillets with a thin coating of grapeseed oil and then season with salt and pepper on both sides. Sear the fillets in the hot pan for 3 to 4 minutes and then turn over. Cook for another 3 to 4 minutes, or until opaque throughout. Remove from the heat and let the fillets rest in the pan for a few minutes.

In a bowl, toss the pea shoots, celery, and julienned truffle together. Add the vinegar and truffle oil and toss just to combine.

Spoon the celery root purée into the center of each of 6 warmed plates. Make a well in the center and place a fillet in the well. Mound the salad on top of the fillets and garnish with shaved truffle.

NOTE: USE A SMALL, SHARP KNIFE OR VEGETABLE PEELER TO SHAVE THE TRUFFLE INTO THIN PIECES THAT YOU CAN THEN JULIENNE INTO VERY THIN STRIPS.

No one denies that salmon and peas is a classic combination. The great James Beard loved them together, but his preference was for the Western version, seasoned with salt and pepper. When Asians pair salmon and peas, they season them differently. Here, I rub miso on the salmon as a light cure. There's no need for any more seasoning, and the result is absolutely amazing. Miso is one of the most remarkable foods I have encountered—it can be part of the meal or act as a seasoning. Want to get more soy in your diet? Try miso.

miso salmon with english pea sauce

SERVES 4

1 cup English pea juice
(see page 166)

Salt and freshly ground pepper to taste

1 tablespoon red miso

2 tablespoons soy sauce

Four 6-ounce salmon fillets,
pin bones removed

2 teaspoons grapeseed oil

Put the pea juice in a small, heavy saucepan and cook, stirring constantly, over low heat until the juice begins to thicken. Remove from the heat and continue stirring for about 3 minutes, or until the juice stops cooking. Season with salt and pepper, set aside, and keep warm.

In a small bowl, whisk the miso and soy sauce together until blended. Smear the mixture on both sides of each salmon fillet. Lay the fillets in a single layer in a shallow glass or ceramic dish, cover with plastic wrap, and refrigerate for 1 hour.

Preheat the oven to 350°F.

Heat a medium ovenproof nonstick skillet over medium heat. Add the oil and sear the fillets for 3 to 4 minutes, or until well browned on the bottom. Turn the fillets over and transfer the skillet to the oven. Roast for 3 to 4 minutes, or until opaque throughout.

Spoon the pea sauce into the center of each of 4 warmed shallow bowls. Put a fillet on top of the sauce in each bowl and serve immediately.

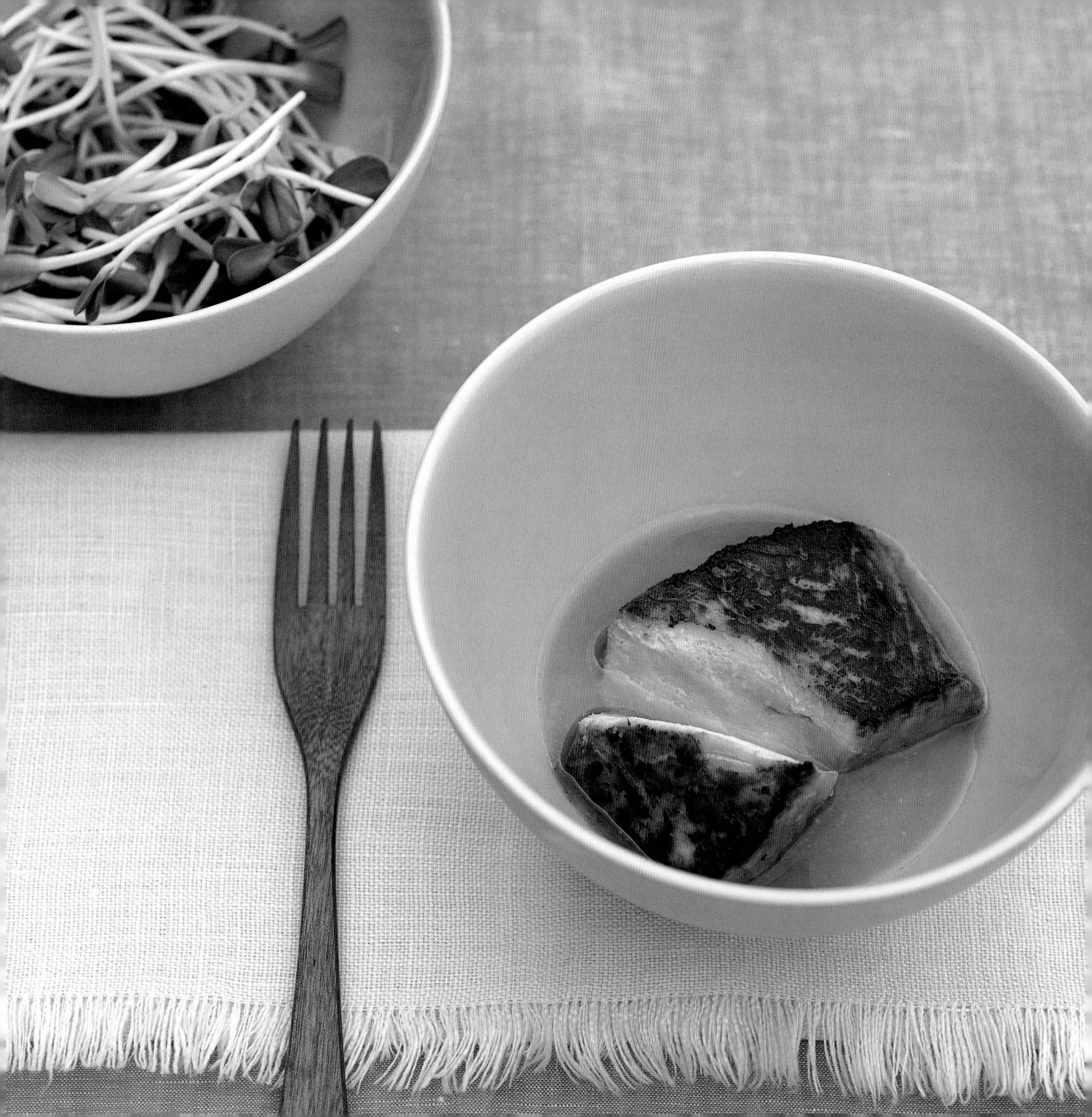

I cook wild salmon when it is available in the spring and summer, but many wish to serve salmon all year round, and more often than not, it's farm-raised. It shows up on nearly every restaurant menu in the country, which is why I think of salmon, not tuna, as "the chicken of the sea." Unfortunately, salmon farms are damaging to the environment, so I advocate using frozen Alaskan salmon when wild salmon is not in season. Frozen salmon, while tasty, is a little more watery and grainy and does not flake well. As luck would have it, I discovered that if I lightly cured frozen salmon, its texture resembled the indescribable dense texture of fresh wild salmon. The cure can vary depending on your preference—here I use Sichuan peppercorns, coriander seeds, and cascabel chilies. The base relies on the correct proportions of salt and sugar. Try Thai flavors such as star anise and lemongrass, the Indian flavors found in garam masala, or Mexican flavors such as cilantro and ancho chilies.

I chose to serve a tahini sauce with the salmon and cauliflower to complement the existing flavors in the dish—and because I noticed that tahini is very often served with cauliflower in Indian and Pakistani restaurants. I tried it; I liked it.

cured salmon with caramelized cauliflower

SERVES **4**

CURED SALMON

1 tablespoon coriander seeds, toasted

1 dried cascabel, Anaheim, or New Mexico chili

1 tablespoon Sichuan peppercorns

½ cup raw cane sugar

¼ cup coarse sea salt or kosher salt

½ teaspoon freshly ground pepper

1¾ pounds skinless, boneless salmon fillet

CONTINUED

TO MAKE THE CURED SALMON: Preheat the oven to 350°F.

In a small dry skillet, toast the coriander seeds over medium heat, shaking the pan, until they are lightly browned and aromatic, 2 to 3 minutes. Transfer to a plate and let cool.

Roast the chili in the oven for 10 to 15 minutes, or until aromatic. Let cool completely. Tear up the chili and put the pieces in a spice grinder. Add the toasted coriander seeds and Sichuan peppercorns and grind them all together until very fine. Some pepper flakes will not break down, which is OK.

In a small bowl, combine the raw sugar, salt, and pepper. Add the ground spice mixture and stir until blended. You should have 1 scant cup of cure. Cut a piece of parchment or waxed paper large enough to cover a baking sheet. Sprinkle half the cure over the center of the paper in roughly the shape of the salmon fillet. Put the

cured salmon with caramelized cauliflower

CONTINUED

TAHINI SAUCE

⅓ cup tahini (sesame paste) at room temperature

3 tablespoons fresh lemon juice

1 garlic clove, crushed through a press

1 teaspoon grated lemon zest

1 teaspoon grated lime zest

¼ teaspoon salt

Dash of cayenne pepper

¼ cup very hot water

CARAMELIZED CAULIFLOWER

One 2¾- to 3-pound cauliflower

About 2½ tablespoons grapeseed oil

Coarse salt and freshly ground pepper to taste

Lemon and lime wedges

Chervil or parsley sprigs for garnish

fish on top and cover it with the remaining cure. Wrap securely in the paper and refrigerate for 2 to 2½ hours.

TO MAKE THE TAHINI SAUCE: Put the tahini in a blender or food processor and add the lemon juice, garlic, lemon and lime zests, salt, and cayenne and blend well. With the machine running, add the water. Transfer to a bowl and let stand for 30 to 60 minutes to allow the flavor to develop.

TO MAKE THE CAULIFLOWER: Remove the green leaves and stem from the cauliflower. Cut off enough of the central core so the vegetable can stand upright. Cut down through the center of the cauliflower to divide the center into 4 slices, each ¾ to 1 inch thick. Reserve the florets from either side for another use (soup or crudités). Gather up all the tiny bits of cauliflower on the cutting board and reserve them.

In a large cast-iron skillet, heat 1 tablespoon of the grapeseed oil over medium-high heat. Add the cauliflower slices in a single layer. Season lightly with salt and pepper. Place another heavy skillet on top of the slices to weigh them down, and press gently. Cook for about 5 minutes, rotating the skillet and pressing down occasionally, until the cauliflower slices are deeply browned on the bottom.

Add the reserved cauliflower bits and drizzle the remaining 1½ tablespoons grapeseed oil over the uncooked side of the cauliflower slices. Turn and cook for 4 to 5 minutes to brown on the second side. Reduce the heat slightly if the cauliflower seems to be browning too fast.

Light a fire in a charcoal grill, preheat a gas grill to medium hot, or preheat the boiler. Scrape most of the cure off the fish, leaving a little for flavor. Cut the fish into 4 equal squares. Grill, skin side up (or broil, skin side down), for 2 to 3 minutes on each side, or until lightly browned on the outside and just slightly translucent in the center. Squeeze about 1 tablespoon *each* of lemon and lime juice over each piece of salmon.

Put a square of cauliflower in the center of each of 4 dinner plates. Arrange the salmon on top. Drizzle the tahini sauce around the fish and garnish with chervil or parsley.

Believe it or not, fish can have the same comforting flavors that conjure up the tastes of mashed potatoes and stuffing. Although we may not consider it too often, most of us love the flavor of celery. It's perfect with cod. When this pan-roasted fish is combined with the smooth flavor of the celery and the earthiness of the potatoes, the flavors remind me of Thanksgiving.

pan-roasted cod with celery and heirloom potatoes

SERVES 4

4 cups low-sodium chicken broth

¼ cup Yukon Gold potato juice (see page 166)

Four 6-ounce cod or haddock fillets

2 teaspoons grapeseed or canola oil

Salt and freshly ground pepper to taste

1 pound unpeeled assorted heirloom potatoes, parboiled until fork tender and halved

6 large shiitake mushrooms (about 5 ounces total), stemmed and thinly sliced

3 shallots, thinly sliced

1 cup ¼-inch-thick diagonally cut celery slices

1 tablespoon fresh thyme leaves

⅔ cup celery juice (see page 166)

Preheat the oven to 450°F.

Put the chicken broth in a medium saucepan and simmer over medium heat to reduce to 1½ cups. Slowly stir in the potato juice until the broth thickens slightly to the consistency of gravy. Add more juice if you prefer a thicker sauce. Remove from the heat.

Rub each cod fillet lightly with oil and season with salt and pepper. Heat a large ovenproof sauté pan or skillet over medium-high heat and sear the fillets for 5 to 6 minutes, or until well browned on the bottom. Turn the fillets over and transfer the pan to the oven. Roast for about 5 minutes, or until the fish is opaque throughout.

Transfer the fillets to a warmed platter, cover loosely with aluminum foil to keep warm, and set aside.

Place the pan over medium heat and add the potatoes, mushrooms, and shallots. Sauté for about 3 minutes, or until the shallots and mushrooms just begin to wilt.

Add the celery and sauté for an additional 30 seconds. Add the chicken sauce and thyme, bring to a simmer, and remove from the heat. Stir in the celery juice and season with salt and pepper to taste.

Spoon the broth and vegetables into 4 warmed shallow bowls and top each with a cod fillet. Serve immediately.

Black sea bass is one of the finest fish for cooking and well worth a search. It's lush, flaky, moist, and succulent. When you steam it over seasoned broth, it takes on the flavor of the broth but retains its own sweetness. Bright green kombu battera (fresh kombu) is cut here to resemble noodles. Sea vegetables are higher in omega-3 and phytonutrients than land vegetables, but too few people eat them, which is a shame because they are so good for us.

steamed black bass with kombu noodles and mushroom dashi

SERVES 4

MUSHROOM DASHI

8 cups water

2 cups sake

1½ cups high-quality soy sauce

2 to 4 large dried kombu leaves, soaked in water for 1 minute

16 carrot batons (4 inches long and ¼ inch wide)

16 daikon batons (4 inches long and ¼ inch wide)

5 to 6 ounces dried shiitake mushrooms

¼ cup dashi flakes

STEAMED BASS

Four 8-ounce black bass or halibut fillets

1 cup sliced Chinese mustard or other mustard greens

24 kombu battera, cut in half lengthwise

Fleur de sel or other coarse sea salt for garnish

TO MAKE THE DASHI: In a large saucepan, combine the water, sake, and soy sauce. Bring to a gentle simmer over medium heat. Add the kombu and simmer for 2 to 3 minutes, or until softened. Add the carrots and daikon and simmer for about 2½ minutes, or until the vegetables begin to soften. Remove the pan from the heat. Discard the kombu and reserve the carrots and daikon.

Add the mushrooms and dashi flakes and let soak while the broth cools to room temperature. Strain, reserving the mushrooms and dashi. Thinly slice the mushrooms and set aside.

Pour 1 cup of the dashi into a small wok. Set a bamboo steamer over the dashi and bring to a simmer over medium heat.

Put the fillets in the steamer, cover, and steam for 6 to 8 minutes, or until the fillets are opaque throughout.

Meanwhile, heat the remaining dashi in a saucepan over medium heat until simmering. Add the reserved carrots, daikon, and mushrooms, and the mustard greens and kombu battera. Return to a simmer and cook for about 1 minute, or until the vegetables are heated through.

Ladle the broth and vegetables into warmed bowls. Arrange the carrots and daikon in a latticelike structure. Lay the bass over the lattice and sprinkle with salt.

One of the things I love most about Creamy Corn Sauce is its versatility. When chilled, it has the consistency of mayonnaise. When I first discovered this, I began thinking of how I could use it cold. Serving it with crab cakes instantly sprang to mind. The sauce lends itself to all different seasonings, and here it blends superbly with lemon and chervil. You will notice I use lemon zest in the crab cakes but then switch to lime juice for the jicama salad. I don't recommend replacing the lemon zest with lime zest, although it might seem logical—lime zest is too distracting for the crab cakes.

crab cakes with papaya and jicama salad

SERVES 6

2 pounds Maryland fresh lump crabmeat, picked over for shell

2 egg whites, lightly beaten

1¼ cups panko or coarse bread crumbs

¾ cup Creamy Corn Sauce (page 156), chilled or at room temperature

¼ cup finely julienned lemon zest

2 tablespoons minced shallots

½ cup fresh chervil leaves

2 tablespoons canola oil

2 ripe papayas, peeled and seeded

1 jicama (about 1 pound), peeled

¼ cup fresh lime juice

Salt and freshly ground pepper to taste

2 tablespoons Red Beet Syrup (page 157)

In a large bowl, combine the crabmeat, egg whites, ¼ cup of the panko or bread crumbs, ½ cup of the corn sauce, the lemon zest, shallots, and chervil. Set the remaining corn sauce aside at room temperature. Using your hands, gently mix just until the ingredients are incorporated. Try to keep the lumps of crabmeat as whole as possible.

Spread the remaining panko or bread crumbs in a flat dish or on a tray. Form the crab mixture into 6 large or 12 small cakes. Press both sides of the crab cakes into the crumbs so that they are lightly coated, or press the mixture into a biscuit cutter depending on the size you want the crab cakes. The cutter can range from 1½ to 2½ inches in diameter. Gently lift the cutter from the cake.

Heat a large sauté pan or skillet over medium heat and add the oil. Using a broad spatula, add the crab cakes and cook for about 5 minutes, or until browned on the bottom. Carefully turn over and cook for about 4 minutes longer, or until browned on the other side and cooked through. Transfer to a plate and cover to keep warm.

Cut the papayas lengthwise into ⅛-inch-wide strips. Stack the strips and cut into long julienne. Repeat with the jicama.

In a medium bowl, combine the papaya and jicama and toss with the lime juice. Season with salt and pepper. Divide the salad among 6 chilled salad plates. Rest 1 large or 2 small crab cake(s) against the salad and garnish by drizzling the remaining corn sauce over the cakes and the beet syrup around the plate.

The key to this dish is the fennel. Since prawns and fennel go well together and fennel and orange taste good together, it's reasonable to expect that all three would taste good together. True! Fennel opened the door to a lovely dish. Because it's near impossible to buy fresh shrimp today, it's important to cook them in their shells. The shells provide some of the flavor the shrimp lose during the inevitable freezing even as they hold in whatever juice exudes from the shrimp. When this same juice weeps on the fennel, the dish sings with mild flavors that are more of a whisper than a shout.

grilled prawns with
fennel and onions

SERVES 6

24 jumbo shrimp (see Note) with heads on (10 or fewer per pound)

½ cup orange-flavored extra-virgin olive oil or unflavored extra-virgin olive oil

Salt and freshly ground pepper to taste

2 large fennel bulbs, trimmed, thinly sliced, and chilled

1 sweet onion, thinly sliced and chilled

¼ cup finely julienned orange zest

¼ cup thinly sliced fresh Thai mint or other mint leaves

Soak 24 wooden skewers in cold water for 30 minutes.

With a pair of scissors or shears, cut through the soft under-shell of each prawn. Spear each prawn with a bamboo skewer through the tail to the small end of the body. This will help keep the prawns from curling during cooking. Lay them in a large dish and drizzle with ¼ cup of the oil. Season well with salt and pepper, cover, and refrigerate for 1 hour.

Light a fire in a charcoal grill or preheat a gas grill to medium.

Grill the skewered prawns on one side for about 5 minutes or until pink. If they seem to be cooking too quickly or burning, move them to a cooler portion of the grill. Transfer them to a plate, cover, and set aside.

In a medium bowl, toss the fennel, onion, orange zest, and mint leaves with the remaining ¼ cup oil. Season with salt and pepper to taste. Mound the salad in the center of each of 6 chilled salad plates. Arrange 4 prawns on each plate, removing the heads, if you wish, before serving.

NOTE: JUMBO SHRIMP ARE OFTEN CALLED PRAWNS (REAL PRAWNS ARE A KIND OF FRESHWATER SHRIMP). BUY THE LARGEST SHRIMP YOU CAN FIND. THOSE LABELED U-10 ARE PREFERRED.

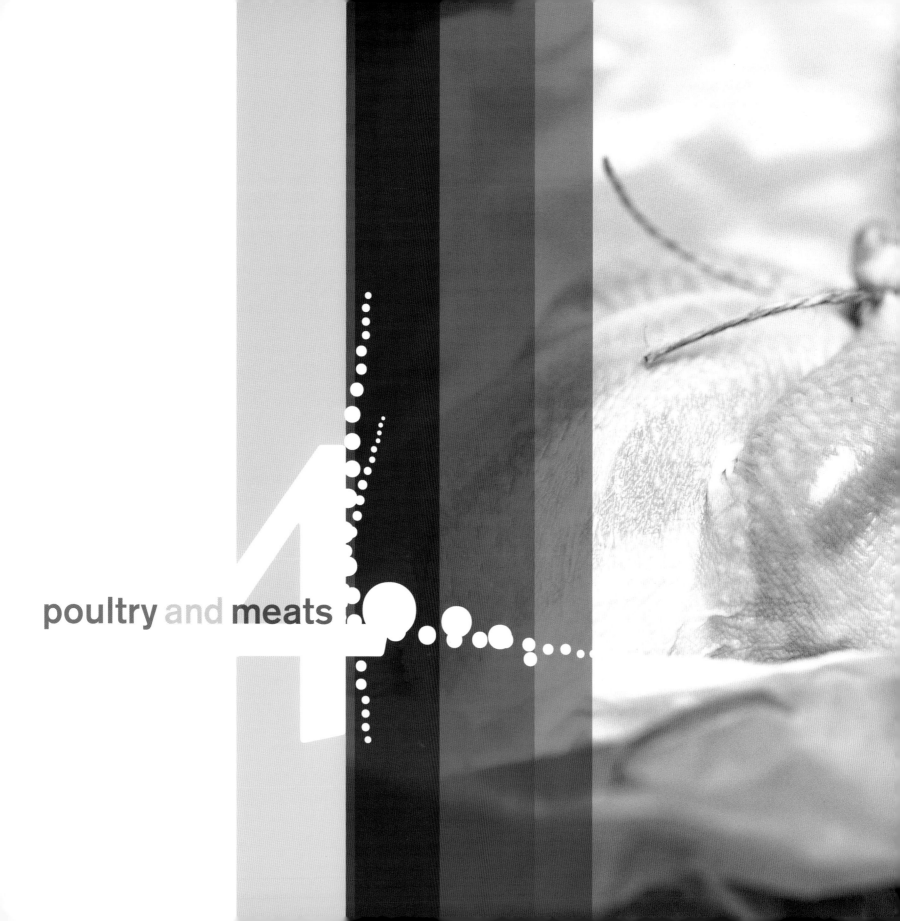

poultry and meats

pistachio-roasted poussin 74

roasted chicken breasts with
dinosaur plum sauce 76

chicken and grilled-corn succotash 77

pan-roasted chicken with heirloom tomatoes
and fresh bay leaves 78

roast turkey with sweet potato gravy
and heirloom squash dressing 80

roast capon with napa cabbage
and autumn pears 84

pan-roasted quail with peach
and porcini mushroom hash 87

coriander breast of duck with
sweet potato sauce 88

mustard-roasted tenderloin of pork
with rutabaga and golden beets 91

grilled leg of lamb with cherries, rhubarb,
and horseradish 94

rack of lamb with pomegranate-date chutney 96

natural beef tenderloin with wild mushrooms
and yukon gold potatoes 99

garlic-grilled strip steak with corn béarnaise 101

bison "cube" steak with fresh figs 103

marinated venison loin steaks with onions
and sweet peppers 104

I love the flavor of nuts with poultry, so I developed this recipe for roast poussins—small, tender chickens—and pistachios. Although they may be hard to find, poussins are well worth searching for, but if you can't locate them use Cornish hens instead. I also prefer Sicilian pistachios in this recipe. They are longer, softer, and more flavorful than more commonly available pistachios, which are fine to use, too. The step of tucking ground pistachios under the skin allows their gentle flavor to permeate the meat.

pistachio-roasted **poussin**

SERVES **4** TO **6**

4 small poussins, fat trimmed 1¼ to 1½ pounds each (the smaller, the better)

1 cup pistachio nuts

3 teaspoons fresh thyme leaves

6 teaspoons grapeseed oil

Coarse salt and freshly ground pepper to taste

¼ cup chopped cipollini or Vidalia onion

2 cups Rich Chicken Stock (page 160)

Preheat the oven to 375°F. Rinse the poussins inside and out and pat dry.

In a spice grinder, grind ½ cup of the pistachios to a powder; add 2 teaspoons of the thyme leaves. Carefully loosen the skin from the poussin breasts and thighs by working your fingers all around between the skin and the meat. Stuff the pistachio mixture under the skin of the breasts and thighs of each bird. Rub the top of each bird with 1 teaspoon of the grapeseed oil to help them brown, season generously inside and out with salt and pepper, and dust with any remaining bits of pistachio. Tuck the wings under the back and tie the legs together.

Use the remaining 2 teaspoons oil to coat a roasting pan just large enough to hold the birds comfortably. Put them in the pan, breast side down. Roast for 15 minutes. Turn the birds over (breast side up) and roast 20 minutes longer. Increase the heat to 425°F and roast for about 10 minutes, or until skin is nicely browned and the juices run clear when the thickest part of a thigh is pierced with a small knife.

Meanwhile, in a small saucepan, combine the onion, stock, the remaining ½ cup pistachios, and the remaining 1 teaspoon thyme. Bring to a boil, reduce the heat, and simmer, uncovered, for 20 minutes.

Transfer to a blender or food processor and purée until smooth. Season with salt and pepper to taste. There should be about 1½ cups the consistency of a thick cream sauce. Serve the poussins with the sauce passed on the side.

This plum sauce is made from fresh plum juice and reduced chicken broth for a complex sauce that requires very little effort. I like to use dinosaur plums, lumpy fruits with light purple, translucent skins, but any large purple-skinned plums will work. This makes a great summer dish served with a green salad tossed with sliced plums. Dress the salad with a little plum sauce, too.

roasted chicken breasts with dinosaur plum sauce

SERVES 4

3 cups plum juice (see page 166), plus 1 dinosaur or other large purple-skinned plum, pitted, peeled, and diced

1 cup low-sodium chicken broth

Salt and freshly ground pepper to taste

4 skin-on boneless chicken breast halves

1 teaspoon grapeseed oil

½ cup baby greens or mixed salad greens

½ small red onion, thinly sliced

2 tablespoons chopped roasted cashews

Strain the plum juice through a fine-mesh sieve lined with cheesecloth or a coffee filter. Gently push the juice through the sieve with the back of a spoon and then let it sit for 5 to 10 minutes before using. Squeeze the cheesecloth to extract juice.

Combine the strained plum juice and chicken broth in a medium nonreactive saucepan over medium heat. Bring to a low simmer, adjust the heat, and cook for about 30 minutes to reduce to the consistency of maple syrup. You should have about 2½ cups of sauce. Season with salt and pepper and set aside.

Preheat the oven to 400°F. Season the chicken breasts with salt and pepper.

Heat the oil in a large ovenproof sauté pan or skillet over medium-high heat. Cook the chicken breasts, skin-side down, for about 5 minutes, or until the skin is crisp. Turn the breasts over and transfer the pan to the oven. Roast for 15 to 18 minutes, or until the chicken are cooked through and their juices run clear when the breasts are pierced with a small, sharp knife. Transfer to a plate and cover loosely with foil.

In a small bowl, combine the diced plum, greens, onion, and cashews. Drizzle some of the plum sauce over the salad, season with salt and pepper, and toss.

Slice and arrange each chicken breast just below the center of each of 4 warmed plates. Divide the salad and rest it against each breast. Drizzle with the remaining plum sauce.

Mom used to mix leftover chicken pulled from the bone with creamed succotash, heat it up, and spoon it over toast. It was the best chicken à la king I ever had. You can make this with leftover roast chicken or freshly sautéed chicken breasts. Either way, once the corn is grilled, it's simple, fast, and great!

chicken and grilled-corn succotash

SERVES 6

1½ pounds skinless, boneless chicken breasts

Salt and freshly ground pepper to taste

2 tablespoons grapeseed oil

¼ cup diced sweet onion

2 pounds fava beans, shelled, blanched, and peeled (see page 158), or 1 cup lima beans or English peas

3 ears fresh corn, shucked, grilled, and kernels cut from cobs (see page 158)

3 large carrots, roasted and cut into ¼-inch dice (see page 166)

3 cups Creamy Corn Sauce (page 156), warmed

Fresh lemon juice to taste (optional)

Cut the chicken into generous bite-sized cubes. Season with salt and pepper.

Heat the grapeseed oil in a large nonstick sauté pan or skillet over medium heat. Sauté the chicken for 2 to 3 minutes, or until seared on all sides.

Add the onion and sauté for 2 to 3 minutes, or until translucent. Add the beans or peas, corn kernels, and carrots and sauté for about 2 minutes, or until heated through.

Remove the pan from the heat, let the contents cool for 30 seconds, and then stir in the corn sauce. Season with salt and pepper to taste. If the corn kernels are extra sweet, temper them with a squeeze of fresh lemon juice. Serve immediately.

There's a lot going on here in what essentially is a very simple recipe. First, I like to use a method called low-temperature sautéing, which means I heat a dry pan over low heat until it's quite hot. I rub oil on the chicken instead of the pan and put the chicken in the hot pan. This prevents the oil from breaking down. I gradually increase the heat as the poultry cooks to let the skin crisp without scorching or drying out the meat.

For the full, rich, and unmistakable "vegetable-and-herb" flavor of this dish, I rely on pure chicken stock, made from only water and bones. This lets you taste the tomatoes, herbs, and chicken all at once, but you can also identify each flavor on its own. The tomatoes provide a full ripeness; the bay leaves, a freshness; and the chicken, a richness. Use whatever tomatoes are ripe and flavorful if you can't find the heirlooms listed below. One last word: Fresh bay leaves are getting easier and easier to find and are well worth looking for. You may want to invest in a fresh bay plant to add to your herb collection. If you can't get them, don't substitute dry bay leaves, which taste more like a hard spice than an herb. Use fresh basil instead.

pan-roasted chicken with heirloom tomatoes and fresh bay leaves

SERVES **4**

8 fresh bay leaves or basil leaves

4 skin-on, boneless chicken breast halves (about 6 ounces each)

4 teaspoons grapeseed oil

Sea salt and freshly ground pepper to taste

8 to 12 Roasted Garlic Cloves (page 159)

8 cups Rich Chicken Stock (page 160)

1 Purple Cherokee tomato, cut into ½-inch-thick slices

1 Big Daddy Sunshine tomato, cut into ½-inch-thick slices

Insert 4 of the bay or basil leaves between the skin and meat of each chicken breast. Cover and refrigerate for 1 hour. Remove the leaves and discard.

Heat a large sauté pan or skillet over low heat.

Rub 1 teaspoon of the grapeseed oil onto the skin of each chicken breast. Lightly season each breast on both sides with salt and pepper and place the breasts, skin side down, in the hot pan. Increase the heat to medium and cook for about 7 minutes, or until well browned on the bottom. Turn the chicken over and pat the browned side with a wadded paper towel to absorb excess fat.

Add the garlic to the pan and sauté until fragrant. Add the stock and simmer for 3 to 5 minutes, depending on the thickness of the chicken breasts, or until opaque throughout. Using tongs, transfer to a warmed plate.

**4 small Green Zebra tomatoes,
cut into ½-inch-thick slices**

**8 yellow pear tomatoes,
halved lengthwise**

**8 red pear tomatoes,
halved lengthwise**

**¼ cup aged balsamic vinegar,
or more as needed (optional)**

Increase the heat to medium-high and cook the stock for about 10 minutes, or until it is reduced and as thick as syrup. Reduce the heat and add the tomatoes. Cook for 1 or 2 minutes, or just until the tomatoes are heated through. Swirl the pan, rather than stirring, so that the tomatoes retain their individual shape and color.

Remove the pan from the heat and add the remaining bay or basil leaves, swirling them into the sauce. Season to taste with salt, pepper, and a splash of balsamic vinegar, if the sauce needs acidity.

Spoon the tomatoes into warmed shallow bowls or deep rimmed plates. Place the chicken breasts over the sauce and serve garnished with the bay or basil leaves.

Classic Thanksgiving dinner is hard to improve upon—a perfectly roasted turkey served with mashed potatoes and gravy is delicious—but it's undeniably rich and fat-laden, which is no fun for anyone with health problems. Organic, free-range turkeys have less fat and more flavor than other turkeys and so are a good choice. Before the turkey reaches the oven, I crack the backbone, which makes it easy to sever the white meat from the dark when the white meat is cooked. This way, it does not dry out.

I serve the bird with squash stuffing and roasted vegetables that have shared its roasting pan and absorbed much of the good turkey flavor. Instead of traditional gravy, I make a sweet potato gravy. The sweet potato juice is naturally starchy, so there's no need for roux as thickener. But don't forget to juice the potatoes early in the day: the liquid must stand for at least 4 hours so that the unwanted starches settle to the bottom.

roast turkey with sweet potato gravy and heirloom squash dressing

SERVES 10 TO 12

12 pounds sweet potatoes, juiced (see page 166)

ROAST TURKEY

One 16-pound organic turkey at room temperature (see note)

Salt and freshly ground pepper to taste

4 cups Rich Chicken Broth (page 160)

24 cipollini or pearl onions

6 to 8 small golden beets, peeled, or 8 small purple-top turnips, peeled

5 large carrots, peeled

Juice the sweet potatoes and set the juice aside.

TO ROAST THE TURKEY: Preheat the oven to 350°F. Rub the cavities and the skin of the turkey with salt and pepper. Use a large, sharp knife to break the back of the turkey. To do this, locate a spot just above where the thighs join the backbone. Insert the knife in a separation between 2 vertebrae and exert enough pressure to just cut through the vertebrae. Take care that the leg-thigh sections remain attached to the turkey with uncut tissue.

Put the turkey in a roasting pan just large enough to hold it. Add 2 cups of the chicken stock and then tent the bird with foil. Roast, basting occasionally, for about 4 hours, or 15 minutes per pound. If the drippings dry up, add more stock.

After 2 hours, remove the foil and add the onions, beets, and carrots. Continue to baste the turkey as the vegetables cook. Check the vegetables occasionally, since one may cook more quickly than another. When the vegetables are tender, transfer them to a warmed ovenproof serving dish and cover to keep warm.

After 3½ hours, begin testing for doneness with an instant-read thermometer. When the breast reaches an internal temperature of 150° to 160°F, remove the bird from the oven and transfer it to a cutting board. Do not turn the oven off.

Cut the skin where the breast meets the thigh. Remove the breast and wings from the rest of the turkey and transfer to a platter. Cover with aluminum foil.

Pour the drippings from the roasting pan into a saucepan before returning the leg and thigh sections (dark meat), sliced side up, to the roasting pan. You should have 5 or 6 cups of drippings. Return the onions to the pan. Continue roasting the turkey until the internal temperature of the meat reaches 165° to 175°F.

MEANWHILE, MAKE THE GRAVY: Carefully remove as much fat as you can from the pan drippings. Cook the defatted drippings over medium-high heat to reduce to 1 cup.

Remove the turkey from the oven. Let the leg-thigh sections rest for 10 to 15 minutes. Pry the thighs backward to loosen them from the backbone. Finish removing the backbone with a sharp knife. Carve the leg-thigh sections and breast. Arrange the turkey meat on a platter with the roasted vegetables.

SWEET POTATO GRAVY

Reserved defatted pan drippings from roast turkey, above

9 cups sweet potato juice (see page 166), above

1-inch piece fresh ginger, peeled and thinly sliced

2 jalapeño chilies, seeded and minced

Salt and freshly ground pepper to taste

Heirloom squash dressing (page 82)

CONTINUED

Strain the settled juice through a fine-mesh sieve, being careful to leave the starch behind. You should have about 6 cups of strained juice.

Pour the strained juice into the roasting pan with the defatted pan drippings. Bring to a simmer over medium heat, stirring to scrape up the browned bits from the bottom of the pan. Transfer to a large saucepan and cook over medium heat to reduce until thickened, 30 to 45 minutes.

Remove from the heat and stir in the ginger and jalapeños. Strain immediately. Season with salt and pepper to taste.

NOTE: A 16-POUND TURKEY SHOULD BE REMOVED FROM THE REFRIGERATOR 1 HOUR BEFORE COOKING. DO NOT LEAVE IT OUT ANY LONGER.

This dressing, baked separately from the bird, has all the good flavor of a traditional stuffing without the fat overload. Because the vegetables are roasted separately, they retain their moisture and flavor. The dressing is moistened by full-bodied reduced turkey or chicken stock—no butter in sight! If you have the stock, make this a day ahead of time.

heirloom **squash** dressing

SERVES **10** TO **12**

CONTINUED

8 cups Rich Chicken Stock (page 160) or turkey stock

One 1-pound loaf black bread, such as pumpernickel, cut into ½-inch cubes

1 large butternut or acorn squash, peeled, seeded, and cut into ½-inch cubes

2 tablespoons grapeseed oil, plus more for coating onions

Salt and freshly ground pepper to taste

2 unpeeled Vidalia or other sweet onions, halved horizontally

3 unpeeled Granny Smith apples, cored and cut into ½-inch cubes

Fresh lemon juice

12 Italian chestnuts, roasted and peeled (see below)

1½ tablespoons minced fresh savory leaves, plus 4 fresh savory leaves, minced

Put the stock in a large pot. Bring to a boil over high heat, reduce the heat to a simmer, and cook for 20 to 30 minutes, or until reduced to 4 cups.

Preheat the oven to 350°F. Spread the bread cubes on a baking sheet and toast, stirring occasionally, just until crisp, about 20 minutes. Transfer to a bowl.

Toss the squash with the 2 tablespoons oil to coat lightly and season with salt and pepper. Spread on a baking sheet and roast for 15 to 20 minutes, or until tender. Transfer the squash to a bowl.

Rub the onions with a little oil and season with salt and pepper. Put them on the baking sheet, cut-side down, and roast for 30 to 35 minutes, or until caramelized and tender. Remove from the oven, leaving the oven on. Peel the onions and cut into ½-inch cubes.

In a large bowl, toss the bread with the squash, onions, apples, lemon juice, chestnuts, and the 1½ tablespoons savory. Slowly add enough reduced stock to moisten the ingredients so that they form a cohesive mixture (you may not need all 4 cups). Season with salt and pepper and spoon into a lightly oiled casserole. To make ahead, cover and refrigerate for up to 1 day. Bake for about 40 minutes, or until hot and crusty. Garnish with the remaining savory.

ROASTING AND PEELING CHESTNUTS: Cut an **X** in the flat side of each chestnut with a small, sharp knife. You will need to apply some pressure to pierce the leathery shell, so take care. Spread them on a baking sheet, **X**-side up, and roast in a preheated 300°F oven for 15 to 30 minutes, or until the skin around the incision starts to curl.

Take a few chestnuts from the oven and let them cool just until you can hold them without burning your fingers. Try peeling these; if they are too tough, roast them a little longer. The roasting time depends on the age and moisture of the nuts.

In most batches, there are always a few chestnuts that refuse to peel. Drop these in simmering water for about 5 minutes. They should now peel easily, although they will not be quite as flavorful as the oven-roasted ones.

Capons are grand birds. They are large enough to be abundant, but are more manageable in size than turkey. When entertaining for four to six people, I find ordinary chicken bothersome—one is not enough, and two are double the trouble to prepare. On the other hand, capons, which are gelded roosters, have plenty of white and dark meat; usually there is enough for leftovers the next day. Plus, while they roast, they perfume the whole house with their comforting aroma. Their rich flavor veers toward being gamy, which makes them delicious with cabbage. I also love to serve them with pears in the autumn when the fruit are just perfect. It really doesn't matter what kind of pears you use, as long as they are ripe. Rock-hard fruit won't do!

roast capon with napa cabbage and autumn pears

SERVES 6

GAME BIRD SEASONING

2 teaspoons freshly ground pepper

2 tablespoons coriander seeds, toasted (see below)

2 green cardamom pods

1 tablespoon fennel seeds, toasted (see below)

1 tablespoon coarsely chopped or torn fresh thyme or savory leaves

1 tablespoon coarse sea salt

In a coffee or spice grinder, combine all the ingredients for the seasoning. Grind to halfway between a medium crack and fine powder.

Preheat the oven to 375°F.

To prepare the capon, use a large, sharp knife to break the back of the capon. To do this, locate a spot just above where the thighs join the backbone. Insert the knife in a separation between two vertebrae and exert enough pressure to make an incision just through the vertebrae. Take care that the leg-thigh sections remain attached to the capon.

Season the capon skin well with the seasoning. Fill the body cavity with the onion, garlic, chervil, thyme, and tarragon.

Choose a roasting pan just large enough to hold the capon comfortably. Arrange the parsnip and carrot halves on the bottom of the pan. Pour the water over the vegetables and place the bird on top. Cover loosely with aluminum foil and roast for about 1½ hours, or until an instant-read thermometer registers 120°F when inserted in the thickest part of the breast. Do not let the thermometer touch bone.

At this point, watch the capon carefully. Continue roasting for about 45 minutes longer, or until the internal temperature reaches 150°F. Baste it occasionally with the pan juices.

Use 2 large spatulas to lift the breast portion of the bird and transfer to a warmed platter. This will be easy because of the cuts made before roasting. Cover the breast loosely with foil and set aside.

Remove the rest of the capon and the parsnips and carrots from the pan. Strain the pan juices into a heatproof glass measuring cup and slightly skim the fat from the surface.

Turn the leg and thigh portion of the capon over and return it to the roasting pan. Continue roasting until the internal temperature of the meat registers 160°F when an instant-read thermometer is inserted into one of the thighs, not touching bone. Transfer to the same platter holding the breast.

Cut the parsnips and carrots into ½-inch-long pieces. Transfer to the roasting pan and add the pear juice, stock, and defatted pan juices. Bring to a rapid simmer over medium-high heat and cook for 15 to 20 minutes, or until reduced by half. Cut 4 ripe pears into wedges, remove the cores, and add them to the reduction. Cover and set aside.

Heat a large sauté pan or skillet over medium-high heat. Add the oil and immediately add the cabbage. Stir-fry the cabbage for a few minutes, or just until it wilts. Add the cloves, salt, and pepper.

Place a mound of cabbage in the center of each of 6 warmed deep plates or shallow bowls. Carve the bird and serve the slices over the cabbage. Spoon the sauce and 2 or 3 pear wedges over the capon and serve.

TOASTING SEEDS AND WHITE SPICES: Spread the seeds or spices in a dry small skillet and toast over medium heat for 2 to 3 minutes, or until fragrant. Light-colored seeds or spices will turn light brown. Shake the pan during toasting to prevent burning. Slide the contents onto a plate to cool and halt the cooking. Toast different kinds of seed and spices separately.

CAPON WITH CABBAGE

One 8- to 10-pound capon

1 large onion, quartered

6 Roasted Garlic Cloves (page 159)

½ cup packed minced fresh chervil

1 bunch thyme

1 bunch tarragon

1 large parsnip, peeled and halved lengthwise

1 large carrot, peeled and halved lengthwise

1½ cups water

2 to 3 ripe pears (about 1 pound), juiced (see page 166), plus 4 ripe pears

1½ cups Ham Hock Stock (page 162)

1 tablespoon orange-flavored oil or unflavored extra-virgin olive oil

1 pound napa cabbage, cored and thinly sliced

1 pinch ground cloves

Salt and freshly ground pepper to taste

Porcini mushrooms are the key to this recipe. They may be hard to get, and you can substitute shiitakes or chanterelles, but for a slam-dunk, use porcini. They have a luscious silken texture and a distinctive fruitiness, which makes them ideal with peaches.

No poultry, not even a boned chicken breast, cooks faster than quail. If you can't find quail, substitute a 1- to 1¼-pound Cornish hen for 2 quail.

pan-roasted quail with peach and porcini mushroom hash

SERVES **4**

PORCINI MUSHROOM HASH

2 teaspoons grapeseed oil

8 porcini mushrooms

8 pearl onions, roasted, peeled, and quartered (see page 166)

½ cup Chicken Glaze (page 161)

12 Russian fingerling potatoes, halved and roasted (see page 166)

2 tablespoons fig syrup or maple syrup

3 very ripe peaches, peeled, pitted, and each cut into 12 wedges

QUAIL

8 semi-boneless quail

Salt and freshly ground pepper to taste

Grapeseed oil for sautéing

Leaves from 1 bunch arugula, torn (about 3 cups)

1 cup torn frisée (curly endive)

1 tablespoon aged balsamic vinegar

1 tablespoon extra-virgin olive oil

Fig or maple syrup for drizzling

TO MAKE THE HASH: Preheat the oven to 350°F.

Heat a medium sauté pan or skillet over medium heat. Add the grapeseed oil, mushrooms, and quartered pearl onions. Sauté for about 5 minutes, or until the mushrooms begin to soften.

Add the chicken glaze and bring to a simmer. Add the potatoes, syrup, and peaches. Simmer for 3 to 4 minutes, or until the hash is nearly dry. Remove from the heat, cover, and set aside.

TO MAKE THE QUAIL: Season the quail with salt and pepper.

Heat a large sauté pan or skillet over medium heat. Dip a paper towel in grapeseed oil and rub the inside of the pan. Add the quail, breast side down, and sauté for 3 to 4 minutes, or until nicely browned. Turn the quail over and continue to cook for 4 to 5 minutes, or until the breast meat feels springy when gently pushed and the meat is cooked through.

In a medium bowl, toss the arugula and frisée together. Toss with the balsamic vinegar, olive oil, and salt and pepper to taste. Divide among 4 plates. Spoon an equal amount of mushroom hash over each salad and top with a roasted quail. Finish by drizzling fig or maple syrup on the rim of the plates.

This recipe defines my style of cooking in a nutshell: The flavors go together beautifully but none gets lost in the execution. The sweet potato base tastes purely of sweet potato; as it cooks, it thickens and the flavor intensifies. Using this all-vegetable base keeps this recipe tasting deliciously earthy. The juice needs to be made at least 4 hours ahead.

coriander breast of duck
with sweet potato sauce

SERVES **4**

SWEET POTATO SAUCE

3½ cups sweet potato juice (see page 166)

2 tablespoons sliced fresh ginger

1 Thai chili, seeded and minced

Fresh lemon juice, coarse salt, and freshly ground pepper to taste

BREAST OF DUCK

3 to 4 tablespoons coriander seeds, toasted (see page 64)

4 skinless, boneless duck breast halves (about 6 ounces each)

Coarse salt and freshly ground pepper to taste

1½ tablespoons minced fresh flat-leaf parsley

4 teaspoons grapeseed oil

CONTINUED

TO MAKE THE SAUCE: Let the sweet potato juice stand for at least 4 hours or up to 6 hours at room temperature. This will allow much of the potato starch in the juice to settle.

Pour the juice through a fine-mesh sieve into a wide, shallow pan, being careful to leave the settled starch behind. Place the juice over medium heat and bring to a gentle boil. Reduce the heat and simmer for 25 to 30 minutes, or until reduced to about 1 cup. During the first 5 or 10 minutes of cooking, additional potato starch will rise to the surface. Skim it off and discard. If using a relatively deep pan, this reduction could take up to 1 hour.

Remove from the heat and stir in the ginger and chili. Stir until the sauce tastes spicy enough, then strain immediately through a fine-mesh sieve. Season with lemon juice, salt, and pepper.

TO PREPARE THE DUCK BREAST: Crush the coriander seeds in a mortar and pestle or grind in a mini grinder, leaving a little texture. Spread the crushed seeds on a plate.

Season the duck breasts liberally with salt and pepper. Gently press the skinned side of each duck breast in the crushed coriander seeds to coat lightly. Sprinkle the parsley over the other side. Turn over again and drizzle 1 teaspoon of oil over the seeded side of each duck breast.

coriander breast of duck
with sweet potato sauce

CONTINUED

Heat a large nonstick skillet over medium-low heat for about 2 minutes. Cook the duck breasts, seeded side down, for 3 minutes. Turn the duck over and cook for 2 minutes longer. Remove from heat and let the duck stand in the hot pan for 3 to 5 minutes for medium-rare. Transfer to a cutting board and cover loosely with aluminum foil to keep warm.

Pour the sweet potato sauce into the same skillet and stir over medium heat, to scrape up the browned bits from the bottom of the pan. Pass the sauce through a fine-mesh sieve. Carve the duck breasts crosswise into thin diagonal slices. Arrange on warmed plates and spoon the sauce around the duck. Serve immediately.

Pork tenderloin is one of the easiest dishes to make at home, yet it is always sophisticated. Pork and mustard are a great pair, and here I rely on mustard seeds rather than prepared mustard to make the flavor statement. I team the dish with rich, roasted root vegetables. Don't mistake turnips for small rutabagas. Although they sometimes are mistakenly called golden turnips, rutabagas are dense, more complex, and much fuller flavored. They taste great with golden beets, and the glace made with their juices is superb.

mustard-roasted tenderloin of pork with rutabaga and golden beets

SERVES **4**

RUTABAGA AND GOLDEN BEET GLACE

1 tablespoon green cardamom pods, or 1 cinnamon stick

4 cups rutabaga juice (see page 166)

4 cups rich Ham Hock Stock (page 162) or Rich Chicken Stock (page 160)

2 cups golden beet juice (see page 166)

1 tablespoon Extra-Virgin O Lemon Oil or unflavored extra-virgin olive oil

Salt and freshly ground pepper to taste

CONTINUED

TO MAKE THE GLACE: Spread the cardamom pods in a single layer in a dry skillet. Toast over medium-high heat for 1½ to 2 minutes, shaking the pan. Do not break the pods open. Transfer to a baking sheet to halt the cooking and cool. If using a cinnamon stick, do not toast it.

In a large saucepan, combine the rutabaga juice, stock, and beet juice. Bring to a simmer over medium heat. Skim any foam that rises to the surface. Reduce the heat to low and cook for 1 to 1½ hours, or until the liquid is reduced to ½ cup and is the consistency of maple syrup. (To cut the time needed for this reduction in half, pour the liquid into a large, shallow skillet instead of a saucepan.)

Remove from the heat and add the toasted cardamon pods. Set aside to steep for 15 minutes. Strain through a fine-mesh sieve into a small bowl. Gradually whisk in the oil until smooth and thick. Season with salt and pepper to taste and set aside until ready to use. Reheat just before serving.

TO PREPARE THE PORK TENDERLOINS: Preheat the oven to 400°F.

Scrub the beets to remove dirt and hairs, but if they have tails, leave them attached. Rub with about 1 tablespoon of the grapeseed oil. Roast for 45 to 60 minutes, or until tender. Do not turn off the oven. (The beets can be roasted up to 1 hour before serving. Wrap them in aluminum foil and reheat with the pork.)

MUSTARD-ROASTED TENDERLOIN OF PORK

2 golden beets

2 tablespoons grapeseed oil

2 tablespoons mustard seeds,
toasted (see page 85)

2 pork tenderloins,
about 12 ounces each

¼ teaspoon coarse sea salt

Freshly ground pepper to taste

GARNISH

2 tablespoons sunflower seeds,
toasted (see page 85)

4 sunflower sprouts, mâche leaves,
pea shoots, or parsley sprigs

Crush the mustard seeds in a spice or coffee grinder, or crush them with the bottom of a heavy pan or the side of a large, heavy knife.

Trim the tenderloins of all fat and silver skin. Season with sea salt and a sprinkling of pepper. Press the cracked mustard seeds firmly into each tenderloin, taking care to cover all sides. Press or rub the remaining 1 tablespoon oil into the tenderloins.

Heat a medium ovenproof sauté pan or skillet over medium heat. Sear the tenderloins on all sides, then place the pan in the oven and roast for about 12 minutes, or until an instant-read thermometer inserted in the thickest part of a tenderloin registers 150°F. Start checking the meat for doneness after 8 to 10 minutes. Remove from the oven and set aside in a warm place.

Rub the skins from the beets and slice each beet in half. Put a beet half in the center of each of 4 warmed plates. Slice each tenderloin on the diagonal into 8 slices. Arrange 4 slices against the beet on each plate. Spoon some glace on each plate and sprinkle with sunflower seeds. Garnish each plate with sunflower sprouts.

While American cooking has come a long way, one dinosaur has survived: lamb and mint jelly. This is a combination I just don't understand. Other than a Twinkie, nothing has ever tasted more manufactured to me than mint jelly. Just as I would never put a Twinkie on a dessert plate, I would never serve leg of lamb with mint jelly—in fact I would never have a jar of it within a Texas mile of my kitchen! But this does not mean I don't recognize that lamb and mint love each other. And I know that nearly everything that mint loves tastes great with lamb, too. Here, I pair cherries with lamb. Delicious. Kumquats are the ideal garnish for their affinity for Middle Eastern spices.

grilled leg of lamb with cherries, rhubarb, and horseradish

SERVES 6

6 pounds sweet cherries, such as Bing, stemmed and pitted

½ cup grated fresh horseradish

One 5½-pound boneless leg of lamb, butterflied

¼ cup high-quality sherry vinegar

1 large stalk rhubarb (about 8 ounces)

1 cup Rich Chicken Stock (page 160)

Salt and freshly ground pepper to taste

2 tablespoons ground sumac or raz al hanout

¼ cup grapeseed oil

4 cups loosely packed mizuna

6 ripe kumquats, or the grated zest of 2 oranges

½ cup 1-inch-long snipped fresh chives

¼ cup loosely packed julienned fresh mint leaves

Measure 2 cups of the pitted cherries and set aside. Juice the remaining cherries in a juicer. Line a fine-mesh sieve with 3 layers of cheesecloth, set it over a bowl, and pour the cherry juice through it. Let the juice drain slowly. Occasionally squeeze the cheesecloth lightly to coax as much juice as possible through the cheesecloth without pressing too hard on the solids. You should have about 4 cups juice.

Transfer the cherry solids from the cheesecloth to a bowl and mix them with about half of the grated horseradish. Rub this over the lamb, covering both sides. Wrap the lamb with plastic wrap and refrigerate for at least 2 or up to 8 hours.

Measure 1½ cups of the reserved cherry juice and set aside. Transfer the remaining juice to a saucepan. Add the remaining horseradish and the vinegar and bring to a simmer. Cook for 20 to 30 minutes, or until the syrup reduces to 1¼ cups. Transfer to a bowl and set aside.

Peel the rhubarb and cut into ⅛-inch dice. In a small saucepan, combine the stock and the reserved cherry juice. Bring to a simmer over medium heat. Cook for 10 to 20 minutes, or until reduced to ¾ cup. Remove from the heat and set aside.

Light a fire in a charcoal grill or preheat a gas grill to medium.

Unwrap the lamb and use a paper towel to wipe the marinade from the meat. Brush the lamb with the reduced cherry syrup and season with salt and pepper.

Grill the lamb for about 7 minutes on each side, or until an instant-read thermometer inserted in the thickest part of the meat reads 135°F. Transfer to a platter, brush with a little more syrup, and sprinkle with the sumac or raz al hanout.

Gradually whisk enough oil into the reserved syrup to make an emulsified dressing. Season with salt and pepper to taste. Add the mizuna, reserved whole cherries, kumquats or orange zest, chives, and mint and toss well.

Divide the salad among 6 plates. Slice the lamb and arrange the slices in a fan on each side of the salad. Drizzle with the rhubarb sauce and serve immediately.

When Heartbeat first opened, we didn't have lamb on the menu, and while I missed it, I wasn't sure how to present it healthfully. Eventually, I decided to serve small racks of lamb with a fresh chutney. I use organically grown domestic lamb because it has a large eye (the meaty part of the chop), which makes it great for roasting or for chops. Any large-eye lamb rack will be fine. Rack of lamb cooks in very little time in a hot oven. I rub the racks with pomegranate molasses and season them with raz al hanout. The result is exceptionally tender, lightly caramelized meat.

rack of lamb with
pomegranate-date chutney

SERVES 4

3 cups Rich Chicken Stock (page 160)

Put the stock in a large saucepan and bring to a boil over high heat. Reduce the heat to a simmer and cook for 25 to 35 minutes, or until reduced to ¼ cup.

2 racks of lamb, 12 to 16 ounces each

3 tablespoons pomegranate molasses

2 teaspoons raz al hanout

Coarse salt and freshly ground pepper to taste

Have the racks trimmed and the ends of the rib bones Frenched by a butcher, if possible. Rub each rack all over with 1 tablespoon of the pomegranate molasses. Season the meaty side with the raz al hanout and a generous sprinkling of salt and pepper. Let the racks stand at room temperature for 30 to 60 minutes.

Pomegranate-Date Chutney (recipe follows) mixed with 2 tablespoons chopped fresh mint

Preheat the oven to 450°F. Choose a heavy roasting pan or shallow gratin dish large enough to hold both racks. Heat in the oven for about 5 minutes, or until hot. Set the racks, bones down, in the pan and roast for 15 to 20 minutes, or until an instant-read thermometer registers 135° to 140°F for medium-rare. Start checking the meat for doneness after the first 10 minutes in the oven. Take care not to overcook.

In a small saucepan, combine the reduced stock with the remaining 1 tablespoon of pomegranate molasses. Stir well. Heat gently until warm.

Transfer the lamb to a cutting board, cover loosely with foil, and let stand for about 10 minutes. Carve into separate chops. Serve with the sauce, and the pomegranate-date chutney mixed with the mint, on the side.

Most chutneys are cooked and cooked, but this one is barely heated so that it tastes intensely of sweet dates and crushed toasted garlic, both of which contribute to its smooth, slightly sticky texture. Folding pomegranate seeds, lime juice, and kumquats into the chutney at the last minute, rather than cooking them for any length of time, provides a real hit of citrus, and the pomegranate seeds just explode in the mouth. Use garam masala if you can't find raz al hanout, which is a mild North African spice mixture that always contains dried crushed rosebuds, among other spices. Literally translated, the name means "head of shop," which is another way of explaining that the spice mixture is made by the proprietor of the store selling it, and while it will be similar to the raz al hanout sold at another shop, no two are ever exactly alike.

pomegranate-date chutney

MAKES ABOUT **2** CUPS

18 large fresh Jordan or Medjool dates, halved and pitted

1 head Roasted Garlic (page 159)

⅓ cup chopped red onion

1 cup Rich Chicken Stock (page 160)

1 red bell pepper, roasted, peeled, and diced (see page 104)

1 yellow bell pepper, roasted, peeled, and diced (see page 104)

2 tablespoons balsamic vinegar

1 tablespoon pomegranate molasses

¼ teaspoon raz al hanout or garam masala

⅛ teaspoon cayenne pepper

4 large kumquats, thinly sliced and seeded, or grated zest and juice of ½ orange

2 tablespoons sliced fresh mint leaves

⅓ cup pomegranate seeds

¼ cup fresh lime juice

Coarsely chop all but 12 of the date halves. Cut the remaining dates into ½-inch pieces and reserve. Squeeze the garlic cloves from the skins. In a medium saucepan, combine the garlic pulp and chopped dates. Add the onion and stock and bring to a simmer over medium-low heat. Cook for about 10 minutes, stirring often, or until the dates are very soft. Use the stirring spoon to mash the dates and garlic to a paste.

Stir in the bell peppers, balsamic vinegar, pomegranate molasses, raz al hanout or garam masala, and cayenne. Simmer for 5 minutes. Remove the pan from the heat and let cool.

Stir in the sliced kumquats or orange zest and juice, mint, pomegranate seeds, and lime juice.

NOTE: THE CHUTNEY CAN BE STORED IN THE REFRIGERATOR FOR UP TO 1 WEEK. DO NOT ADD THE MINT IF YOU PLAN TO REFRIGERATE THE CHUTNEY, BUT INSTEAD STIR IT IN AS YOU USE THE CHUTNEY.

When we first opened Heartbeat, we had a hard time deciding whether to serve beef, but in the end I decided to include it. After all, I'm a healthy guy and I love beef! So do many other people, and if you don't eat it often, it fits into a healthful diet.

Beef has tremendous culinary significance and there are numerous ways to prepare it. Poaching is one of these, as in the classic French dish *boeuf à la ficelle.* Before you say "yuck!" to poached beef, remember that tenderloin is exceptionally tender meat and nothing maintains its lovely texture better than poaching. Poached meat is missing the characteristic browned crust we have come to expect with beef, so we make a reduced sauce to serve with the meat.

natural beef tenderloin with wild mushrooms and yukon gold potatoes

SERVES 4

8 cups Rich Beef or Veal Stock (page 161)

8 cups Rich Mushroom Stock (page 165)

8 dry-packed sun-dried tomatoes

8 small to medium Yukon Gold potatoes

Grapeseed oil for coating, plus 1 teaspoon

Salt and freshly ground pepper to taste

12 shiitake mushrooms, stemmed and thinly sliced

4 Roasted Garlic Cloves (page 159) plus 3 Roasted Garlic Bulbs, split (page 159)

4 shallots, sliced very thin

1 tablespoon coarsely chopped fresh flat-leaf parsley

1 teaspoon fresh thyme leaves

1 teaspoon minced fresh chives

4 fillets naturally fed beef tenderloin (6 to 7 ounces each), tied along their length

½ cup Buttermilk Sour Cream (page 157)

Put the beef or veal stock in a large pan and bring to a boil over high heat. Reduce the heat to a simmer and cook for 25 to 35 minutes, or until reduced to 3 cups. Repeat with the mushroom stock. Put the sun-dried tomatoes in a bowl and add enough beef or veal stock to cover by an inch or two.

Let the 2 stocks and the tomato-stock mixture cool, then refrigerate each one separately. Let the tomatoes soak for 1 hour. Drain, reserving the stock. Chop the tomatoes and set aside. Return the tomato soaking liquid to the container of beef or veal stock.

Preheat the oven to 450°F.

Scrub the potatoes and pierce them in several places with a small, sharp knife. Coat them with grapeseed oil and lay in a roasting pan in a single layer. Sprinkle with salt and pepper. Roast for about 1 hour, or until tender. Wrap in foil and set aside.

Heat a medium saucepan over medium heat. Add 1 teaspoon grapeseed oil and then the mushrooms. Sauté for about 2 minutes, or until soft.

CONTINUED

natural beef tenderloin with wild mushrooms and yukon gold potatoes

CONTINUED

Pour 1 cup beef or veal stock and 1 cup mushroom stock into the saucepan. Add the garlic cloves, tomatoes, and sliced shallots and bring to a rapid simmer. Cook for about 20 minutes, or until reduced to 1 cup. Stir in 1½ teaspoons of the parsley, ½ teaspoon of the thyme, and ½ teaspoon of the chives. Season with salt and pepper to taste. Cover to keep warm.

Pour the remaining beef or veal stock and mushroom stock into a saucepan large enough to hold the fillets without crowding. Add the fillets, which should be submerged in the stock. Bring to a simmer over medium heat. Add the garlic bulbs and simmer for about 10 minutes, or until fragrant.

Reduce the heat to medium-low, add the fillets, and simmer for 5 to 7 minutes for rare meat, 7 to 9 minutes for medium-rare, and 9 to 11 minutes for medium. Lift the fillets from the poaching liquid and set aside to rest for about 5 minutes. Cut each fillet into 3 slices.

Pierce the top of each potato with a paring knife. Use your fingers to squeeze each potato gently so that it splits and fluffs. Fill each with 1 tablespoon of buttermilk sour cream. Arrange 2 potatoes side by side in the center of each of 4 warmed plates. Lean 3 slices of beef against each potato. Spoon some sauce over each plate and garnish with the remaining herbs.

All steaks taste good with a classic béarnaise sauce, a variation of a particularly unhealthful mother sauce called hollandaise, made with butter and egg yolks. Béarnaise is hollandaise seasoned with a reduction of vinegar, tarragon, wine, and shallots. Once again, our Creamy Corn Sauce comes to the rescue. We developed a sauce made with fresh tarragon, shallots, and vinegar that is a culinarily sound and tasty accompaniment for grilled red meat.

garlic-grilled strip steak with corn béarnaise

SERVES 6

GARLIC-GRILLED STEAK

2 cups Roasted Garlic Cloves (page 159)

¼ cup fresh thyme leaves

2 tablespoons salt

1 tablespoon freshly cracked pepper

Six 8- to 10-ounce boneless
New York strip or shell steaks

CORN BÉARNAISE

1 tablespoon grapeseed oil

1 tablespoon minced shallots

¼ cup plus 1 tablespoon minced
fresh tarragon

¼ cup cider vinegar

1½ cups Creamy Corn Sauce
(page 156)

Mound the garlic cloves onto a cutting board and sprinkle with the thyme, salt, and pepper. Use the flat side of a large knife to mash the garlic into a paste.

Rub both sides of each steak with a generous amount of garlic paste. Lay the steaks in a shallow glass or ceramic dish, cover tightly with plastic wrap, and refrigerate for at least 1 hour or up to 8 hours.

Light a fire in a charcoal grill or preheat a gas grill to medium.

TO MAKE THE BÉARNAISE SAUCE: Heat the grapeseed oil in a small sauté pan or skillet over medium heat. Add the shallots and cook for about 5 minutes, or until translucent. Add the ¼ cup tarragon and cook for about 30 seconds longer. Add the vinegar and cook for a few minutes, or until reduced by half.

Strain through a fine-mesh sieve into a bowl. Stir in the creamy corn sauce. Cover and set aside to keep warm.

About 15 minutes before grilling, lift the steaks from the dish and scrape off most of the garlic paste and let them sit at room temperature. Sear the steaks on the hot grill for 2 minutes and then turn. Sear for another 2 minutes and turn again. Grill for 7 to 9 minutes per side for medium-rare steak, 9 to 11 minutes for medium.

Transfer the steaks to a platter. Let rest for 3 minutes. Fold the 1 tablespoon tarragon into the corn béarnaise and serve with the steak. Reheat the sauce gently, if necessary.

Even chefs like to play with words, which is how I came up with the name of this recipe. Cube steak is tough meat, pounded thin and barely edible. Bison strip steak, also called buffalo, is tender and succulent. When we were holding a series of tea-and-savory-food-pairing tastings at Heartbeat, I created this dish to pair with smoky bao jong tea, a kind of oolong tea. The challenge was to cook the steak in a portion size that was appropriate for a multitasting event. I cut the strip steaks into small cubes, which was logical, but they still were tricky to serve on a small plate with no knife and fork. I cut them into smaller cubes and then reassembled them into the original small steak, which was very easy to eat. Because the dish had become all about cubes, I call it "cube" steak.

bison "cube" steak with fresh figs

SERVES **4**

½ cup dry red wine

Four 12-ounce New York strip bison steaks, 1½ to 2 inches thick, at room temperature

4 to 8 teaspoons grapeseed oil

Salt and freshly ground pepper to taste

¼ cup fig syrup or maple syrup

4 fresh figs, cut into quarters

4 sprigs watercress

In a small saucepan, bring the wine to a boil over high heat. Reduce the heat and simmer the wine for about 25 minutes, or until reduced to 2 tablespoons.

Cut each bison strip steak into 4 equal square or rectangular pieces. Rub both sides of the steaks with grapeseed oil and season generously with salt and pepper.

Sear the steaks in a large nonstick skillet over medium heat for about 1½ minutes on each side, or until lightly browned. You might find it easier to use 2 skillets.

In a small bowl, whisk the reduced wine syrup and fig syrup together. Drizzle each steak with all but about 2 tablespoons of the wine mixture. Cook for 2 to 3 minutes, turning constantly, so that the syrup glazes the meat. Cook about 2 minutes longer for rare, or 4 to 5 minutes for medium-rare.

Transfer the steaks from the pan to a cutting board. Let them rest for about 3 minutes, or until cool to the touch. Cut each steak into small cubes. Reassemble the cubes into the shape of the original steaks, pressing them together to adhere, and place each on a warmed plate.

Arrange the fig quarters on each plate and garnish with watercress. Drizzle the remaining wine syrup over each plate and serve.

Onions and peppers are a classic accompaniment to grilled steaks, their pungency and sweetness acting as a perfect foil for the richness of the meat. Trouble is, the vegetables often are sautéed in copious amounts of butter or oil. When you pair them with steak—even relatively lean venison—any hopes of a healthful meal go out the window. I address this by cooking the roasted peppers and onions lightly in a small amount of oil in a sauté pan set directly on the grill. Venison loin steak is a treat worth having, particularly if you serve it with these simply prepared onions and peppers. If you prefer, serve beef tenderloin steaks instead.

marinated venison loin steaks
with onions and sweet peppers

SERVES 6

PEPPER MARINADE

½ cup molasses

½ cup balsamic vinegar

½ cup Roasted Garlic Cloves (page 159)

1 branch fresh rosemary

½ small Thai chili, thinly sliced, or
1 teaspoon red pepper flakes

1 teaspoon freshly cracked pepper

MARINATED VENISON LOIN STEAKS

Six 1-pound venison loin steaks, bone in

6 red and yellow bell peppers

Salt and freshly ground pepper to taste

3 tablespoons grapeseed oil

1 large Vidalia or other sweet onion,
cut into ¼-inch-thick slices

In a small, heavy saucepan, combine all the marinade ingredients and bring to a simmer over medium heat. Cook for about 10 minutes, stirring occasionally. Remove from the heat. Set aside and let cool to room temperature.

Lay each steak flat on the counter and tie each one horizontally so that the meat forms a tight, round package. You will need 6 pieces of kitchen twine, each measuring about 18 inches long.

Spread half the marinade over the bottom of a nonreactive casserole or deep baking pan just large enough to hold all 6 steaks snugly but without crowding. Arrange the steaks in the pan and coat with the remaining marinade. Cover and refrigerate for at least 3 hours or up to 5 hours.

Remove the steaks from the marinade and place them on a double thickness of paper towels to dry.

Light a fire in a charcoal grill or preheat a gas grill to medium.

Set the peppers over the hottest part of the grill and cook until they begin to char. Turn with tongs and continue grilling until the peppers are charred on all sides. Stand by the grill during this time—the peppers cook quickly. Using tongs to turn them prevents them from splitting open. Transfer immediately to a container just large enough to hold them. Cover tightly with plastic wrap and let the peppers cool to the touch. Rub the charred skin off the peppers. Remove the seeds and ribs from the peppers. Cut the peppers into strips.

About 15 minute before grilling, remove the steaks from the refrigerator and let sit at room temperature. Season the steaks with salt and pepper and brush with half the oil. Grill for 7 minutes on one side. Turn and grill for 7 minutes longer on the other side. Turn one more time and grill for about 2 minutes longer for rare steak. Grill for 1 to 2 minutes longer for medium-rare. Take care when turning the steaks so that the grill marks on the meat are perpendicular to the grate.

Transfer the steaks to a warmed platter and remove the twine.

Place a medium sauté pan or skillet on the hottest part of the grill. Put the remaining 1½ tablespoons oil and the sliced onions in the pan and cook, stirring, for about 5 minutes, or until the onions are lightly browned. Add the pepper strips and cook for about 2 minutes, or until heated through.

Serve the steaks on warmed large plates with the grill marks showing. Carefully spoon the pepper and onions over half of each steak so that the grill marks are clearly visible.

vegetarian **entrées** 5

sweet potato and root vegetable gratin 108

winter vegetable stew 110

sweet pea, corn, and mushroom risotto 113

roasted vegetables with sweet corn and
fire-roasted sweet pepper sauce 115

vegetable lasagne 116

Although some people believe that gratins require butter, milk, cream, or cheese for texture and moisture, it just isn't so. Many vegetables, particularly roots, have sufficient starch and texture for a wonderful, rich-tasting gratin. This one is made only of vegetables, moistened with just a little olive oil. I serve it with Sweet Potato Sauce to add color and bring out the flavor of all the root vegetables and mild greens tossed with oil and seasonings.

sweet potato and root vegetable gratin

SERVES 6

1 tablespoon extra-virgin olive oil

One large rutabaga (about 1 pound), peeled and thinly sliced

Salt and freshly ground pepper to taste

1 pound russet potatoes, peeled

1½ pounds sweet potatoes, peeled and thinly sliced

1 cup shredded Vidalia onions

1 pound large parsnips, peeled and thinly sliced

1 tablespoon minced fresh herbs, such as flat-leaf parsley, thyme, chives, and/or chervil

1 cup Sweet Potato Sauce (page 88)

Preheat the oven to 350°F. Rub an 8½-by-12-inch casserole with olive oil.

Overlap half the rutabaga slices on the bottom of the casserole, making sure the slices do not overlap by more than ½ inch. Sprinkle lightly with salt and pepper.

Thinly slice 1 of the russet potatoes lengthwise and shingle the slices over the rutabaga. Season lightly with salt and pepper. Slice the potatoes as you use them to prevent them from discoloring and so that they retain their starch and nutrients.

Overlap the sweet potato slices over the russet potato. Season with salt and pepper.

Spread about ⅓ cup of the onions over the sweet potato slices, then overlap the parsnips over these.

Repeat the process, ending with sweet potato slices. Spray lightly with a little vegetable-oil cooking spray, season with salt and pepper, cover tightly with aluminum foil, and bake for 40 to 50 minutes.

Remove the casserole from the oven and uncover. Spray lightly with a little more oil. Sprinkle with the minced herbs. Return, uncovered, to the oven for 15 to 20 minutes, or until the top layer is nicely browned. Remove from the oven. Let set for 10 to 15 minutes before slicing and serving.

Heat the sauce gently and serve the gratin with a little sauce drizzled over each serving.

This dish is a perfect vegetarian solution for Thanksgiving. The stew is cooked in a big pumpkin, which makes for a completely natural and edible serving vessel. You carve the pumpkin down to the level of the stew as you serve the stew. It has all the warm and comforting flavors of Thanksgiving, and you get to participate in a carving ceremony!

winter vegetable stew

SERVES **8**

<table>
<tr><td>SPICE MIX</td><td>In a small bowl, stir all the spice mix ingredients together.</td></tr>
</table>

SPICE MIX

²/₃ **cup raz al hanout**

¼ **cup raw cane sugar**

1 tablespoon kosher or coarse sea salt

Freshly ground pepper to taste

SQUASH SAUCE

2 tablespoons grapeseed or extra-virgin olive oil

1 to 2 cups cubed butternut or similar squash

¼ **cup diced onion**

4 cups Roasted Vegetable Stock (page 163)

Salt and freshly ground pepper to taste

Raw cane sugar (optional)

CONTINUED

In a small bowl, stir all the spice mix ingredients together.

TO MAKE THE SAUCE: Heat the oil in a medium saucepan over medium heat. Sauté the squash and onion for about 5 minutes, or until the onion softens.

Add the vegetable stock and bring to a slow simmer. Cook for 15 to 20 minutes, or until the squash is tender when pierced with a fork. Season to taste with the spice mix, salt, pepper, and sugar, if necessary.

Transfer the vegetables and stock to a blender or food processor and puree until smooth. If using a blender, you may have to do this in batches. Return to the saucepan, cover, and keep warm. If the sauce cools before it's time to add it to the other vegetables, heat it very gently over low heat until just hot. Do not let it boil.

Preheat the oven to 400°F.

Cut the top off the pumpkin as though you were going to make a Halloween jack-o-lantern. Seed and scrape the inside of the pumpkin. Clean and reserve the seeds. Rub the lid and the inside of the pumpkin with ¼ cup of the spice mix. Wrap both the lid and the pumpkin completely in aluminum foil. Bake for 45 to 55 minutes, or until the pumpkin is fork-tender.

Spread the rutabaga cubes on a lightly oiled baking pan and roast for about 30 minutes, or until fork-tender. Spread the squash and turnip cubes on a baking sheet and roast for 15 to 20 minutes, or until fork-tender.

winter vegetable stew

CONTINUED

VEGETABLE STEW

One 4- to 6-pound sugar pumpkin

One 4-ounce rutabaga,
peeled and cut into 1-inch cubes
(about 1 cup)

1 pound butternut or similar squash,
peeled and cut into 1-inch cubes

One 4-ounce turnip,
peeled and cut into 1-inch cubes
(about 1 cup)

8 ounces cipollini onions

8 ounces red pearl onions

2 tablespoons extra-virgin olive oil

¼ cup thinly sliced leeks

3 cinnamon sticks, toasted (see Note)

½ teaspoon freshly grated nutmeg

½ jalapeño chili,
seeded and finely minced

3 to 4 large Yukon Gold potatoes,
steamed until tender, peeled,
and cut into 1-inch cubes

2 large Peruvian blue potatoes or
Yukon Gold potatoes, steamed until tender,
peeled, and cut into 1-inch cubes

½ cup coarsely minced fresh herbs,
such as flat-leaf parsley,
thyme, chives, and/or chervil

8 thick slices Russian black or
walnut-raisin bread, lightly toasted

Spread the cipollini and pearl onions on a lightly oiled baking sheet and roast for 8 to 10 minutes, or until softened. Transfer the onions to a bowl and let cool. When cool to the touch, peel the onions.

Meanwhile, heat a large saucepan over medium heat. Add the olive oil and sauté the leeks, onions, cinnamon sticks, nutmeg, and jalapeño until the leeks begin to melt. Add the roasted rutabaga, squash, and turnip and cook until heated through. Add the hot squash sauce and the Yukon Gold and Peruvian potatoes and bring to a simmer. Remove from the heat, remove the cinnamon sticks, and sprinkle with the herbs. Stir them gently into the stew.

Remove the pumpkin from the oven and stand it upright. Ladle the stew into the cavity of the pumpkin.

Lay a slice of toast in the bottom of 8 warmed soup bowls. Sprinkle a little of the spice mix on the rim of the pumpkin. Use a carving knife to cut thin slices off the pumpkin rim. Arrange the slices around the bread, then ladle the stew over the bread.

Sprinkle the freshly cut rim of the pumpkin with more spice mix, and sprinkle the stew with more coarsely chopped herbs. Repeat the process until the stew and pumpkin are gone.

You may have a little leftover pumpkin, but not to worry! Purée it with some spice mix and brown sugar and use as you would canned pumpkin to make pumpkin pie.

NOTE: TO TOAST THE CINNAMON STICKS, HEAT A SMALL SKILLET OVER MEDIUM HEAT UNTIL HOT. ADD THE CINNAMON STICKS AND COOK, SHAKING THE PAN, FOR ABOUT 1 MINUTE UNTIL FRAGRANT. TRANSFER TO A PLATE TO COOL.

Risotto lends itself to many flavors and ingredients and always results in an abundant heartiness. This one is especially welcome in the early fall when corn is still good and mushrooms are easily available. I use Roasted Corn Stock here, which is made with scraped corn cobs, and then I finish the risotto with corn juice. The corn juice finishes the risotto with a delectable creaminess and flavor.

sweet pea, corn, and mushroom risotto

SERVES 6

6 tablespoons extra-virgin olive oil

2 tablespoons diced shallots

2 cups Carnaroli, Arborio, or Vialone Nano rice

6½ cups Roasted Corn Stock (page 164)

2 tablespoons sliced shallots

5 to 6 ounces chanterelle mushrooms, quartered (about 2 cups)

1 tablespoon water

2 cups fresh corn kernels (about 4 large ears)

2 pounds sweet (English) peas, shelled and blanched

1½ cups corn juice (see page 166)

Salt and freshly ground pepper to taste

3 tablespoons sliced fresh tarragon or chervil leaves

3 tablespoons sliced fresh chives

Heat 4 tablespoons of the oil in a very large saucepan over medium heat and sauté the shallots for about 5 minutes, stirring, or until translucent. Add the rice and cook, stirring constantly, for 2 to 3 minutes, or until opaque. Do not let the rice brown.

Add about 2 cups of the stock. Cook, stirring constantly, until the stock is absorbed by the rice. Add another cup of stock and cook, stirring and adding stock, a cup or so at a time, until all but ½ cup of the the stock is absorbed. Reserve the ½ cup of stock. The entire process will take 20 to 25 minutes.

Spread the risotto on a baking sheet, cover with parchment paper, and set aside to cool to room temperature.

Heat the remaining 2 tablespoons oil in the same saucepan and add the sliced shallots. Sauté over medium-high heat until the shallots begin to brown lightly. Add the mushrooms and water and cook for about 5 minutes, or until the mushrooms soften. Add the corn kernels, sauté for about 2 minutes, and then add the peas, the remaining ½ cup roasted corn stock, and the risotto.

Cook for about 3 minutes, stirring constantly but gently, until the risotto heats and absorbs the stock. Add the corn juice and cook for 3 to 4 minutes, stirring, until the risotto is creamy. Season with salt and pepper to taste.

Spoon the risotto into 6 warmed bowls. Garnish with tarragon or chervil and chives and serve immediately.

When I was a cook, I was disappointed when chefs would respond to requests from vegetarian diners with the same boring combination of steamed broccoli, snow peas, and cauliflower. I vowed that when became a chef, I would come up with some good, balanced vegetarian recipes. This dish includes an interesting array of vegetables, which are paired with complementary sauces.

roasted vegetables with sweet corn and fire-roasted sweet pepper sauce

SERVES **8**

1 Delicata squash (about 2 pounds) cut into 8 wedges and roasted (see page 166)

1 acorn squash (about 2 pounds) cut into 8 wedges and roasted (see page 166)

24 Brussels sprouts

6 tablespoons grapeseed oil

Salt and freshly ground pepper to taste

2 ears corn, shucked, each cut into 4 pieces

4 red bell peppers, roasted, peeled, and halved lengthwise (see page 104)

8 portobello mushrooms, gills scraped off

1 tablespoon coarsely grated garlic

1 pound mixed greens, such as kale, spinach, mustard, and chard, stemmed

1 cup Creamy Corn Sauce (page 156)

¾ cup Fire-Roasted Sweet Pepper Sauce (page 156)

¼ cup water

Preheat the oven to 375°F. Lightly coat the roasted squashes and Brussels sprouts with 1 tablespoon of the oil. Season with salt and pepper and spread on a baking sheet. Use 2 sheets, if necessary. Roast for 20 to 25 minutes, turning once, until tender.

Lightly coat the corn and bell peppers with 2 tablespoons of the grapeseed oil and season with salt and pepper. Spread on a baking sheet and roast for about 15 minutes, turning frequently, until cooked through. Remove from the oven, cover, and set aside. With the second roasting, the peppers caramelize and their flavor deepens further.

Preheat the broiler. Use 1 tablespoon of the grapeseed oil to brush the mushrooms and season with salt and pepper. Spread on a baking sheet and broil about 3 inches from the heat source, turning once, for 3 minutes, or until cooked through. Remove from the broiler.

Heat the remaining 2 tablespoons of the oil and the grated garlic in a large sauté pan or skillet over medium heat, and sauté the garlic until golden brown. Increase the heat to high and immediately add the greens. Sauté, tossing constantly, until the greens wilt. Season with salt and pepper, remove from the heat, and cover.

In a small saucepan, heat the corn sauce over medium heat. In a small saucepan, combine the pepper sauce and water and heat gently over medium heat. Drizzle the warm corn sauce and pepper sauce decoratively over 8 large plates. Arrange each of the vegetables on top of the sauces and serve immediately.

There is something comforting about the aroma of a baking lasagne that rivals the smell of a roasting chicken. The trouble is, for anyone with an intolerance for cow's milk cheese, home-cooked lasagne is a spectator sport. By pre-roasting and grilling the vegetables, I have created a rich, satisfying vegetable lasagne. While this sounds like a hassle, it's worth it—the flavors of the vegetables intensify and the texture of the casserole is lush and moist.

vegetable lasagne

SERVES 6 TO 8

1 cup tomato sauce

⅓ cup tomato paste

2 tablespoons extra-virgin olive oil

One 14- to 16-ounce package lasagna noodles, cooked and drained

1 large eggplant, cut lengthwise into ¼-inch-thick slices and grilled (see Notes)

3 cups oil-packed sun-dried tomatoes, drained and coarsely chopped

8 large portobello mushrooms, stemmed, grilled, and cut into thin slices (see Notes)

1 large sweet onion, cut into thin slices

¼ cup loosely packed julienned fresh basil leaves

Salt and freshly ground pepper to taste

1½ cups Fire-Roasted Sweet Pepper Sauce (page 156)

Preheat the oven to 350°F.

In a medium saucepan, stir the tomato sauce and tomato paste together and bring to a simmer over medium heat. Remove from the heat.

Lightly coat the bottom of a 9-by-13-inch baking dish with 1 tablespoon of the olive oil. Lay a single layer of noodles (about one-fourth of the noodles) in the bottom of the dish.

Brush the noodles with a scant one-fourth of the tomato sauce and then top with half the eggplant, half the sun-dried tomatoes, half the mushrooms, and half the onion. Sprinkle with one-fourth of the basil and season with salt and pepper to taste.

Ladle a thin layer of sweet pepper sauce over the vegetables, and then sprinkle with about one-fourth of the crumbled goat cheese.

Begin layering again with lasagne noodles and brush with more tomato sauce and another quarter of the crumbled goat cheese. Layer with more lasagna noodles and brush with both tomato sauce and pepper sauce.

Top with layers of half the zucchini, half the carrots, and half the parsnips. Sprinkle with a little basil and season with salt and pepper to taste. Spread with more tomato and pepper sauce.

12 ounces fresh white goat cheese, crumbled (about 2½ cups)

2 large zucchini, cut lengthwise into thin pieces

4 large carrots, roasted and cut lengthwise into thin pieces (see page 166)

3 large parsnips, roasted and cut lengthwise into thin pieces (see page 166)

5 to 6 ounces aged goat cheese, thinly sliced (1 to 2 cups)

At this point, layer half the aged goat cheese over the lasagne.

Repeat the process with the remaining ingredients, beginning with more noodles and then layering the vegetables, cheese, sauces, basil, and salt and pepper as described above.

Spread the remaining tomato sauce over the top of the lasagne and finish with a final layer of aged goat cheese. Sprinkle with the remaining 1 tablespoon oil. Cover with aluminum foil and bake for 45 to 50 minutes, or until bubbling hot. Remove the foil and bake for about 15 minutes longer, or until the goat cheese is lightly browned. Remove from the oven and let sit for about 15 minutes before serving.

NOTES: TO GRILL THE EGGPLANT, BRUSH THE SLICES LIGHTLY WITH OLIVE OIL AND SEASON WITH SALT AND PEPPER. GRILL OVER MEDIUM-HOT COALS OR ABOUT 4 INCHES FROM A PREHEATED BROILER, TURNING ONCE OR TWICE, FOR 6 TO 10 MINUTES, OR UNTIL LIGHTLY BROWNED.

TO GRILL THE MUSHROOMS, BRUSH BOTH SIDES OF THE CAPS WITH OLIVE OIL AND SEASON WITH SALT AND PEPPER. GRILL THE MUSHROOMS, TOP SIDE DOWN, OVER MEDIUM COALS OR ABOUT 4 INCHES FROM A PREHEATED BROILER FOR ABOUT 2 MINUTES, OR UNTIL THE MOISTURE WELLS UP WHERE THE STEM WAS REMOVED. TAKE CARE THE MUSHROOMS DON'T BURN. IF THEY BEGIN TO DARKEN, MOVE THEM TO A COOLER PART OF THE GRILL, OR TURN DOWN THE HEAT (IF USING A GAS GRILL). TURN OVER AND GRILL FOR ABOUT 1 MINUTE LONGER, OR UNTIL SOFTENED.

6 side dishes

grilled summer peppers with fresh bay leaves   120

grilled asparagus   122

"marshmallow" corn   123

garlic mashed potatoes   124

root vegetable and wild mushroom hash   125

lightly salted edamame   127

garlic wilted spinach   128

"wok"-charred bok choy   129

Summertime's sweet bell peppers are a riot of lively color and flavor, and I serve them as often as possible, particularly when I fire up the grill. These are grilled and then left to mingle with the bay leaves, but I reheat them quickly before serving to intensify their flavor. This also brings out the wonderful flavor of the bay leaves. If you are not in the habit of using fresh bay leaves, you will become a fan as soon as you try them. Don't substitute dried bay leaves for fresh here—use finely shredded fresh basil instead.

grilled summer peppers
with fresh bay leaves

SERVES 6

3 large red bell peppers

3 large yellow bell peppers

2 tablespoons
extra-virgin olive oil

12 fresh bay leaves or
basil leaves

Salt and freshly ground pepper
to taste

Light a fire in a charcoal grill or preheat a gas grill to medium.

Put the peppers over the hottest part of the grill and cook until they begin to char. Turn with tongs and continue grilling until the peppers are charred on all sides. Stand by the grill during this time—the peppers cook quickly. Using tongs to turn them prevents them from splitting open. Transfer immediately to a container just large enough to hold them. Cover tightly with plastic wrap and let the peppers cool to the touch.

Peel the blackened skin from the peppers, scraping them gently with a small knife. Take care to keep the peppers whole. Coat the peppers with the oil and transfer to a bowl large enough to hold them snugly.

Tuck the bay leaves among the peppers so that the leaves come in contact with each pepper. Let sit for 1 hour. If using basil leaves, cut them into thin shreds for better flavor and presentation.

When ready to serve, lay the peppers on a cool part of the grill and heat for 20 to 30 seconds on each side. Season with salt and pepper and serve.

Fresh asparagus explodes with moisture and sweet, green flavor. When I lived in Wisconsin, I used to forage for wild asparagus, which was amazing. If you have an opportunity to pick it, you have to do it. Just picked, it's best raw. I put asparagus in the category of vegetables that do best with minimal cooking. Quick grilling is one of the best treatments.

grilled asparagus

SERVES 4

24 asparagus spears with medium-thick stalks (about 2 pounds total)

1 tablespoon grapeseed oil

Salt and freshly ground pepper to taste

Light a fire in a charcoal grill or preheat a gas grill to medium.

Coat the asparagus spears with the oil. Lay the spears directly on the grill. Grill for 1 to 2 minutes, or until well marked from the grill. Using tongs, roll the spears over and cook the other side for 1 minute, or until grill marked. Alternatively, cook them in a grill pan over high heat.

Season to taste with salt and pepper and serve.

I remember picking sweet corn on my grandparents' farm when we were kids. My brothers and I got so thirsty out in the hot field, we'd rip open an ear and eat it then and there, drinking in its sweet moisture. The taste of "Marshmallow" Corn reminds me of that fresh corn, straight from the field: indescribably sweet and moist. No doubt, many purists will object to this treatment of a favorite summertime treat, but it's worth trying. The corn loves the sweet milk, and as it cooks, the air around the grill fills with an aroma that can only be described as toasted marshmallow. Not surprisingly, kids love this!

"marshmallow" corn

SERVES 6

6 ears yellow corn,
thick outer husks removed

6 cups whole milk

¾ cup raw cane sugar

1 vanilla bean,
halved lengthwise

Pull the remaining husks on the corn back from each ear and remove the silk. Pull the leaves back up over the ears of corn. Cut about ½ inch off the end of each ear to allow the corn to absorb the milk.

Put the corn in a casserole dish just large enough to hold it in a single layer (use 2 casseroles if necessary). Pour 4 cups of the milk over the corn. (If using 2 dishes, pour 2 cups into each dish.)

Put the remaining 2 cups milk, the sugar, and the vanilla bean in a small saucepan and heat over low heat, stirring constantly, until the sugar dissolves.

Pour the milk over the corn and shake gently to make sure the sweet milk mixes with the rest of the milk. Set aside at room temperature to soak for 1 to 2 hours. The longer the corn sits, the sweeter it "gits."

Light a fire in a charcoal grill or preheat a gas grill to medium.

Grill the corn on the edge of the grill where the heat is not too intense. Cook, turning constantly, for 15 to 20 minutes, or until the corn is heated through. If the husks char, don't worry.

Shuck the corn and serve immediately.

Mashed potatoes, the American comfort food, should be satisfying from the first bite to the last—and if correctly made, they are. Don't cook the potatoes until they fall apart; instead, the chunks should hold together and just slip off a knife when pierced. Boiling them is destructive, so simmer them gently. If mashed potatoes are sticky, the potatoes were over-cooked and overwhipped. If they are grainy and chunky, they were undercooked.

garlic mashed potatoes

SERVES 4 TO 6

4 large russet potatoes (about 2 pounds), peeled and cut into 2-inch pieces

1 teaspoon salt, plus more to taste

2 to 3 tablespoons warm low-fat milk

2 tablespoons Roasted Garlic Cloves (page 159)

2 tablespoons extra-virgin olive oil

Freshly ground pepper to taste

Put the potatoes in a medium saucepan and add just enough water to cover them. Add the 1 teaspoon salt and bring to a simmer over medium heat. Do not boil. Cook for 12 to 15 minutes, or until the potatoes are just tender enough to slide off a paring knife when pierced. Drain well and return to the pan. Set the pan over low heat and cook for 1 to 2 minutes to dry the potatoes out.

Remove from the heat and lightly mash the potatoes with a fork just to break them up. Stir in the milk, mashed garlic, and olive oil. Run the potatoes through a food mill or mash them with a potato masher to the desired consistency. Season with salt and pepper to taste and serve immediately.

When I think of root vegetables I think of strength and the earth, just as tomatoes make me think of the sun. Mushrooms, which also are earthy, love root vegetables, so I use them here with parsnips and carrots. The trick to getting the best flavor from root vegetables is to roast them. Come fall, my mom and I roasted nearly all of our vegetables, even before we sautéed or otherwise cooked them. We even served roasted vegetables chilled. Preroasting them in their skins holds in nutrients and keeps them moist. Parsnips are a puzzle. I have found that in any group of people, only one or two in twenty even knows what they are—but when they are properly cooked, their flavor and texture are amazing: a cross of sweet potato, carrot, and roasted marshmallow.

root vegetable and wild mushroom hash

SERVES 4 TO 6

4 parsnips (about 1 pound total), scrubbed, poached for 15 minutes, and cooled

18 baby carrots or 6 medium carrots (about 1 pound total), scrubbed

5 tablespoons extra-virgin olive oil

Coarse salt and freshly ground pepper to taste

12 ounces shiitake mushrooms, stemmed and cut into ¼-inch-thick slices

1 teaspoon dried thyme

Halve the parsnips lengthwise. If using baby carrots, leave them whole; if using medium carrots, split them lengthwise and then crosswise in half. Cut the vegetables with 1 tablespoon of the oil and season lightly with coarse salt and pepper.

Place the carrots on a baking sheet and roast for about 10 minutes. Add the parsnips in a single layer and roast for 10 to 15 minutes longer, or until the vegetables are lightly browned and tender but still firm. Transfer to a cutting board. Let cool slightly and then cut into ½-inch-thick pieces.

In a large skillet, heat 1 tablespoon of the oil over medium-high heat. Add the shiitakes and sauté, tossing often, for about 3 minutes, or until tender and lightly browned.

Add the roasted carrots and parsnips and the remaining 3 tablespoons oil. Sauté for about 2 minutes, or just until the hash is heated through. Season with the thyme and salt and pepper to taste.

Everyone is talking about soy these days, especially women, but I've noticed frustration as people try to get enough soy in their diets without overdosing on tofu. Edamame are the fresh soybeans that, converted into curd, become tofu. I simmer them gently and then toss them with salt, which I love as a snack. In Japan, edamame are a way to say "welcome." For me, they are fast becoming an obsessive snack—once you make the recipe, you'll see why.

lightly salted edamame

SERVES 6 TO 8

⅓ cup salt

2 pounds fresh or frozen
edamame

Coarse sea salt or
fleur de sel to taste

Fill a stockpot with water, add the salt, and bring to a boil over high heat. Add the edamame, reduce the heat to a simmer, and cook for about 3½ minutes for fresh and 4½ minutes for frozen.

Drain and transfer to a bowl just large enough to hold the edamame and keep them warm while serving. If the bowl is too large, the beans will cool off before you want them to. Toss with salt and serve.

When I ate at Etats Unis, a restaurant in New York City, shortly after it opened, I was impressed by a salmon dish that was served mounded with garlic-infused spinach. And we're not talking about a delicate hint of garlic, but a good, satisfying dose. The very next day I started to fool around with ways to make a similar spinach side dish—and here it is.

garlic wilted spinach

SERVES 4 TO 6

8 garlic cloves, thinly sliced
(about 2 packed tablespoons)

2 tablespoons grapeseed oil

12 ounces spinach,
stemmed

2 tablespoons
extra-virgin olive oil

Salt and
freshly ground pepper
to taste

Put the garlic slices and grapeseed oil in a medium sauté pan or skillet and set it over medium heat. The garlic will begin to cook slowly at first and then quickly as the pan heats. Stir occasionally to make sure the garlic does not stick or burn and that it cooks evenly. When golden brown, raise the heat to high and add the spinach and olive oil.

Cook, stirring constantly, for 2 to 3 minutes, or until the spinach wilts. Season to taste with salt and pepper and serve immediately.

If you've ever wondered how to serve bok choy, the white-stalked Chinese cabbage with the crinkly green leaves, this is one of the best methods. The smaller the bok choy, the more tender. Nothing fancy here—just fresh flavors cooked in a wok over high heat.

"wok"-charred bok choy

SERVES **6**

6 baby bok choy,
each about 9 inches long

¼ cup grapeseed oil

12 very thin slices fresh ginger

4 garlic cloves,
thinly sliced

Salt and
freshly ground pepper
to taste

Split each bok choy in half lengthwise. The bulb of the bok choy takes longer to cook than the stalks and leaves. Slit the bulb horizontally.

Choose a wok, sauté pan, or skillet large enough to hold all 12 pieces or use 2 smaller pans. Heat the oil in the pan over medium-high heat until it begins to ripple. Add the ginger and garlic slices and sauté for a few seconds until the garlic begins to brown. Move the pan slightly off the burner so that the handle is not exposed to the heat. The garlic will brown first, so push it to the cooler side of the pan and continue to cook the ginger until it turns brown and crisp.

Push the ginger to the cool side of the pan and add the bok choy halves, cut side down and with the bulb ends in the hottest part of the pan. Cook for 2 to 3 minutes, or until well browned. Turn and season with salt and pepper.

Spoon the garlic and ginger over the bok choy. Cook for 2 to 3 minutes more, or until the bok choy is just tender and browned on the bottom. Serve immediately.

breakfast

squash pancakes with fig syrup   133

breakfast vegetable hash   134

steel-cut oatmeal with apricots and mission figs   135

pastel omelet with shiitake mushrooms,
goat cheese, and fresh herbs   137

granola   138

Part of the challenge of creating healthful recipes was figuring out how to use less flour for all those people who have trouble digesting wheat. I looked around, noted the leftover starch pulp from juicing squash and sweet potatoes, and decided to fool around with using it to replace flour. This recipe calls for a little flour, but I have experimented with no flour at all—just egg whites—with good success.

The pancakes are almost like mini soufflés, and many who have tried them can't believe I cook them on a griddle. If you don't have a griddle, a nonstick sauté pan or skillet works well. You will need a thin-bladed spatula and patience when you tackle these, and no doubt the first few pancakes will fail. Keep going; you'll get the hang of it, and these are worth it.

squash pancakes with fig syrup

SERVES **4**

12 ounces butternut or Hubbard squash, peeled, seeded, and cubed (about 3 cups)

¼ cup cake flour (not self-rising)

½ cup apple juice

2 large egg whites

1 to 2 teaspoons fig or maple syrup, plus more for serving

Salt and freshly ground pepper to taste

1 tablespoon grapeseed oil

Juice the squash (see page 166), reserving the pulp. You should have ¼ cup pulp and ½ cup juice. Put the squash pulp in a medium bowl and sprinkle with the flour. Using your fingertips, gently squeeze the pulp and cake flour together until they are just blended. Add the squash and apple juices, and stir gently until blended.

In a large bowl, beat the egg whites until soft peaks form. Add the 1 to 2 teaspoons syrup and beat until stiff, glossy peaks form. Stir one-third of the egg whites into the squash batter. Season with salt and pepper. Gently fold the lightened batter into the egg whites. Be careful not to blend the mixture completely. The more gently you treat the egg whites, the higher the pancakes will rise. You should have about 2⅓ cups batter.

Heat a large nonstick sauté pan, skillet, or griddle over medium heat. Rub the oil over the surface of the hot pan with a paper towel. Ladle about ¼ cup of the batter into the pan and cook for about 4 minutes, or until just set. Using an oiled thin-bladed metal spatula, very gently turn the pancake over and cook for 1½ to 2 minutes, or until done. The pancakes will be very soft and light.

As it sits, the batter will separate. Stir or fold it gently before cooking the rest of the pancakes. Serve the pancakes overlapped on heated plates and drizzled with syrup.

Although most people don't think of vegetables as breakfast food, there is no reason not to. This hash provides nutritional value as well as interest to the first meal of the day. It's great as a side dish or topped with poached eggs. Use whatever root vegetables you have on hand and roast the vegetables up to 3 days ahead and refrigerate (see page 166 for roasting information). That way you can make this when you're ready.

breakfast **vegetable** hash

SERVES **4**

2 tablespoons grapeseed oil

1 sweet potato, roasted, peeled, and cut into ½-inch dice

2 purple potatoes (about 3 ounces each), roasted, peeled, and cut into ½-inch dice

1 large or 2 medium carrots, roasted, peeled, and cut into ½-inch dice

1 turnip, roasted and cut into ½-inch dice

1 parsnip, roasted and cut into ½-inch dice

1 small Vidalia onion or other mild, sweet onion, roasted and diced

About ¼ cup mixed minced fresh herbs, such as parsley, thyme, chives, and/or chervil

Salt and freshly ground pepper to taste

2 cups leftover mashed potatoes

Heat 1 tablespoon of the oil in a 12-inch nonstick sauté pan or skillet over medium-high heat. Add the roasted vegetables and sauté for 3 to 4 minutes, or until they start to crisp and turn brown. Sprinkle with the herbs and season with salt and pepper to taste.

Mix the vegetables with the mashed potatoes. Taste and adjust the seasoning.

Heat the remaining 1 tablespoon of oil in a nonstick skillet. Form the vegetables into 4 cakes. Each cake will require about 1⅓ cups hash. Sauté for 1½ to 2 minutes per side, or until lightly browned. Serve immediately.

I like the texture of steel-cut Irish or Scottish oats, although old-fashioned rolled oats will also do. I sweeten the oatmeal with fruit instead of sugar for its nutritive benefits, but if I am in the mood for a little more sweetness, I'll add a spoonful of honey or fig syrup. When I want a big breakfast, I eat this alongside scrambled eggs.

This oatmeal is great after a morning workout. After I kayak on Long Island Sound some mornings, I eat a big bowl of this before I head for work and find I can keep going well into the afternoon.

steel-cut oatmeal with apricots and mission figs

SERVES 6

3 cups water

½ teaspoon salt

1 cup Irish or Scottish steel-cut oatmeal or old-fashioned rolled oats

1 cup apricot nectar or apple juice

About 3 ounces dried apricots, cut into ¼-inch dice (about ⅔ cup)

About 3 ounces small dried Mission figs, each quartered lengthwise (about ⅔ cup)

1 cup Granola (page 138)

In a medium saucepan, bring the water and salt to a simmer over medium-high heat. Stir in the oatmeal, reduce the heat, cover, and cook at a low simmer for about 25 minutes.

Stir in the apricot nectar or apple juice and cook for 10 minutes more, or until the liquid is absorbed but the oatmeal is still moist. Stir in the apricots and figs, and if the oatmeal seems dry, add more nectar. Cook about 5 minutes longer, or until heated through and the consistency you like.

Serve in warmed bowls, topped with generous sprinklings of granola.

No matter how you cook them, egg whites alone will never be as firm or have the richness of whites and yolks cooked together. Because of this, I add 1 yolk to 2 whites (you could also use 1 yolk for 3 whites), which produces a lovely pale yellow omelet. Goat cheese, mushrooms, and fresh herbs are naturals with eggs and with each other, and a little goat cheese goes a long way toward adding flavor. If you want, use low-fat goat cheese for this brunch or light lunch dish.

pastel omelet with shiitake mushrooms, goat cheese, and fresh herbs

SERVES **2**

12 shiitake mushrooms, stemmed

Salt for sprinkling, plus more to taste

2 large eggs

4 large egg whites

1 tablespoon mixed minced fresh herbs (such as parsley, thyme, and chives)

Freshly ground pepper to taste

1 tablespoon canola oil

3 tablespoons crumbled goat cheese

Preheat the broiler. Wipe the mushroom caps with a damp paper towel. Set the mushrooms on a small baking sheet, coat lightly with nonstick vegetable-oil spray, and sprinkle with salt. Broil, gill side down, and about 4 inches from the heat source, for 2 minutes. Turn over and broil for about 2 minutes longer, or until lightly browned. Transfer to a cutting board and let cool to the touch. Cut into slices.

In a medium bowl, combine the eggs, egg whites, and half the herbs. Whisk vigorously until well blended and frothy. Season with salt and pepper to taste.

Heat a 10-inch nonstick skillet over high heat and add the oil. Immediately pour in the eggs and scatter the mushrooms over them. Rapidly stir with a folding motion for about 2 minutes, concentrating on moving the eggs from the outside of the pan to the center until the omelet begins to set.

Reduce the heat to low and continue stirring and folding for another 2 minutes or so until the omelet sets. Remove from the heat and sprinkle the goat cheese evenly over the omelet.

Roll the omelet onto a warmed platter, garnish with the remaining herbs, and serve immediately.

As a chef with five children, I try to involve my kids in cooking as much as I can, mainly as a way to make sure they eat good food. Granola is something they can make with me and then customize as they like, choosing their favorite dried fruit or deciding on toasted walnuts instead of hazelnuts, for example. My kids don't really like plain yogurt, which is what I eat this with, but even if they eat granola with flavored yogurt, I know they are getting a healthful meal.

granola

MAKES ABOUT 7 CUPS; SERVES 6 TO 8

1 cup (4 ounces) hazelnuts

1 cup (4 ounces) unblanched almonds

1 cup (4 ounces) raw cashews

⅓ cup canola oil

½ cup maple syrup

¼ cup packed brown sugar

Grated zest of 1 orange

1 vanilla bean, split lengthwise

2 cups old-fashioned rolled oats

7 to 8 ounces dried fruit, such as apricots, raisins, plums, peaches, or apples, diced

2 cups goat's milk yogurt or other plain yogurt, drained (see page 48)

½ cup tupelo or other mild-tasting honey

3 cups goat's milk or cow's milk for serving (optional)

Preheat the oven to 325°F.

Spread the hazelnuts, almonds, and cashews in a single layer on a baking sheet and toast for about 8 minutes, or until lightly browned and fragrant. Remove from the oven, leaving the oven on. Transfer to a large plate and let cool. With a rolling pin, crush the nuts until coarse.

In a medium bowl, stir the oil, maple syrup, brown sugar, orange zest, and vanilla bean together. Add the oats and stir gently to coat. Spread the mixture on a baking sheet and toast for 15 to 20 minutes, stirring every few minutes to encourage even browning.

Remove from the oven and let cool on the pan. Transfer the granola to a bowl and toss with the dried fruit.

Divide the granola among 6 breakfast bowls. Top with yogurt and drizzle with honey. Serve milk on the side, if desired.

desserts

fresh figs with semolina toast
and rhododendron honey 142

flourless hazelnut cakes with chocolate centers 144

almond polenta cake with orange cream 146

champagne mangos with raspberry coulis
and cardamom shortbread 148

cardamom shortbread 150

sweet potato brûlée 151

My mother taught me the value of fresh, perfectly ripe fruit and vegetables, and few fruits pleased her as much as ripe peaches. She used to slice peaches in high summer and lay them on toast drizzled with honey. This gave me the idea for using other fruit this way. When I found soft, almost overripe figs in a greenmarket in Sonoma, California, and thick, rich semolina bread in a nearby bakery, I returned to a friend's restaurant kitchen and created a very simple dessert for his customers. Everyone loved it, and so I have incorporated it into my repertoire of desserts. The kind of honey is important. Rhododendron honey will blow you away with its full but light flavor, but use any light honey you particularly like, such as tupelo, orange blossom, or raspberry. When the honey and the figs collide, the flavor is fantastic. The bread does not have to be semolina bread; use sourdough or a country loaf instead, but make sure it has a good, dense texture when toasted.

If you want to substitute peaches for figs, go ahead; you will need 6 peaches for the recipe. But if you can, try figs. They are one of the most incredible fruits—look for light to dark green figs in early summer, and then very dark Mission figs in the fall. They should feel soft when you buy them and must be eaten right away. Their edible seeds are soft and moist, their flavor, dark, deep, and intense.

fresh figs with semolina toast
and rhododendron honey

SERVES 4

6 very ripe dark figs, quartered

6 very ripe green figs, peeled, if necessary, and quartered

1 tablespoon balsamic vinegar

Salt and freshly ground pepper to taste

4 large slices semolina or other dense-textured bread, cut 1 inch thick (preferably from a 2-pound loaf)

2 tablespoons extra-virgin olive oil

2 tablespoons rhododendron or other mild honey

In a medium bowl, gently toss the figs with the vinegar. Season with salt and pepper and set aside.

Brush each slice of bread on each side with the olive oil. Put the slices of bread in a large sauté pan or skillet and cook over medium heat, turning the bread until crisp and lightly browned on both sides.

Place each slice of toast in the center of each of 4 plates. Top with the figs and drizzle with honey.

A lot of people watch what they eat so that they can indulge in a dessert such as this one—and it's quite an indulgence! Remember, it's not what you eat on a given day that really matters, it's how you conduct your eating for the entire week, month, and year.

This is a good, dense, moist dessert that's delicious with sliced bananas and the best chocolate sorbet you can find. I suggest Häagen-Dazs. The praline paste and butter make a big-time flavor statement. You can find praline paste at supermarkets or specialty foods stores, sold in plastic-wrapped rolls. If you make these cakes ahead of time, wrap them each tightly in plastic and store them at room temperature for a day or in the refrigerator for 2 to 3 days. For a variation, make the cake without the chocolate centers.

flourless hazelnut cakes with chocolate centers

SERVES **8**

CHOCOLATE CENTERS

4 ounces semisweet or bittersweet chocolate, coarsely chopped

4 tablespoons unsalted butter

5 large egg yolks

4 tablespoons sugar

TO MAKE THE CHOCOLATE CENTERS: In a double boiler melt the chocolate and butter over simmering water. Immediately remove from heat and remove the top of the double boiler from the bottom so that the chocolate does not overheat. Let cool to lukewarm.

In the bowl of an electric mixer set on medium speed, beat the egg yolks and 2 tablespoons of the sugar until doubled in volume. Fold the yolk mixture into the cooled chocolate with a rubber spatula.

In a clean bowl of an electric mixer set on medium speed, beat the egg whites until frothy. Increase the speed to medium-high and add the remaining sugar until stiff, glossy peaks form. Fold into the chocolate mixture. Set aside in a warm place.

TO MAKE THE CAKES: In the bowl of an electric mixer set on medium-high speed, cream the butter and ¾ cup plus 2 tablespoons of the granulated sugar for 3 to 4 minutes, or until light and fluffy. Add the egg yolks one at a time, beating well after each addition and scraping down the sides of the bowl as needed.

Add the salt and praline paste and beat until smooth and creamy. Remove the bowl from the mixer. Add the flour and fold it into the batter with a rubber spatula. Set aside.

HAZELNUT CAKES

4 tablespoons unsalted butter
at room temperature

1 cup plus 2 tablespoons granulated sugar

5 large egg yolks

Pinch of salt

2¾ ounces praline paste

1 cup hazelnut flour, sifted

5 large egg whites

Sliced bananas for serving

Raw sugar for garnish

High-quality chocolate sorbet
for serving (optional)

In a clean bowl of an electric mixer set on medium speed, beat the egg whites until frothy. Increase the speed to medium-high and add the remaining ¼ cup granulated sugar until stiff, glossy peaks form.

Fold about a third of the meringue into the batter to lighten it. When it is just incorporated, fold in the remaining meringue.

Spoon the mixture into the muffin cups, filling each about half full. Spoon the chocolate mixture into a pastry bag fitted with a plain tip and pipe chocolate into each muffin cup. Insert the tip of the pastry bag into the hazelnut batter and pipe the chocolate into it so that the lighter-colored batter comes up and over the chocolate filling and each cup is about three-fourths full.

Bake for 20 to 25 minutes, or until the tops are golden and spring back when pressed.

Serve warm, with sliced bananas dusted with raw sugar. Caramelize the sugar using a small blowtorch or a preheated broiler, and serve with chocolate sorbet, if desired.

I love this recipe because it hints of the connection between my mother's Southern cooking heritage, which she passed on to me, and Italian country food, some of the finest in the world. Although I grew up in Illinois, I was raised on grits. One bite of this reminded me of my mother's warm corn bread, which she served with honey and fruit. A little bit of this dense, awesome cake goes a long way.

almond polenta cake with orange cream

SERVES 8 TO 10

1 cup (2 sticks) unsalted butter at room temperature

1 cup granulated sugar

Grated zest of 1 lemon

3 eggs

1 teaspoon pure vanilla extract

½ teaspoon almond or orange extract

2 cups almond flour (see Notes)

⅔ cup polenta or finely ground yellow cornmeal

1½ tablespoons cake flour

¾ teaspoon baking powder

Pinch of salt

Preheat the oven to 375°F. Butter an 8-inch round springform pan or an 8-inch cake pan that is 2 inches deep. Line the bottom with a round of parchment paper or waxed paper. Butter and flour the paper and the sides of the pan. Tap out the excess flour.

With a heavy-duty electric mixer fitted with the paddle attachment, beat the butter until smooth. Gradually beat in the granulated sugar and then the lemon zest until light and creamy. Beat in the eggs, one at a time. Mix in the vanilla and almond or orange extract. Add the almond flour and beat until blended.

In a medium bowl, combine the polenta or cornmeal, cake flour, baking powder, and salt. Whisk gently to blend. In several increments, fold the dry ingredients into the butter mixture. The batter will be thick. Scrape into the prepared pan and smooth the surface.

Bake for 35 to 40 minutes, or until the top is golden brown and the edges begin to pull away from sides of pan. Start checking the cake for doneness after 30 minutes. If it begins browning before the center is cooked, cover loosely with aluminum foil. Let cool in the pan for 10 minutes, then unmold and let cool completely on a wire rack. The cake will sink as it cools.

ORANGE CREAM

8 ounces (1 cup) mascarpone cheese at room temperature (see Notes)

¼ cup sifted confectioners' sugar

1 tablespoon grated orange zest

Confectioners' sugar for dusting

Orange segments or fresh strawberries for serving

MEANWHILE, MAKE THE ORANGE CREAM: In a small bowl, combine all the ingredients. Blend gently with a rubber spatula until well mixed. Cover and refrigerate. Remove from the refrigerator 30 minutes before using. Blend with a spatula before spreading on the cake.

With a large serrated knife, carefully cut the cooled cake in half horizontally to make 2 layers. Fill with the orange cream. Dust the top lightly with confectioners' sugar. Serve with orange segments or strawberries.

NOTES: IF YOU CANNOT FIND ALMOND FLOUR, PUSH 1½ CUPS BLANCHED ALMONDS THROUGH THE GRATING DISK OF A FOOD PROCESSOR. SWITCH TO THE METAL BLADE AND ADD ½ CUP OF GRANULATED SUGAR; PULSE REPEATEDLY UNTIL COARSE. LET THE MACHINE RUN UNTIL THE ALMONDS ARE FINELY GROUND. IF YOU USE THIS IN THE RECIPE, BEAT ONLY ½ CUP OF SUGAR WITH THE BUTTER. YOU CAN ALSO GRIND BLANCHED ALMONDS IN A BLENDER.

IF YOU PREFER, INSTEAD OF MASCARPONE CHEESE, WHIP 1 CUP HEAVY CREAM WITH THE CONFECTIONERS' SUGAR, ORANGE ZEST, AND ½ TEASPOON VANILLA EXTRACT UNTIL STIFF.

Fruit desserts can be as elegant as more traditional desserts. Sweet fresh raspberries, which may not even need the sugar syrup, offset the vibrant orange of mango in this simple, beautiful, and healthful dessert. The hint of cardamom in the shortbread ties the dessert together. Even if you don't serve the entire dessert, try the shortbread; it's great to have on hand to serve with tea or coffee. Champagne mangos are smaller than ordinary mangos. If you can't find them, choose the best fruit you can find and make sure it's ripe before slicing. A ripe mango will give when pressed and smell fragrant.

champagne mangos with raspberry coulis and cardamom shortbread

SERVES 4

2 cups fresh raspberries

2 to 4 teaspoons
Raw Sugar Simple Syrup (page 157)

2 Champagne mangos, or
1 large regular mango, cut from the pit,
peeled, and sliced (see Note)

Four 4-by-3-inch
Cardamom Shortbread cookies
(page 150)

4 tablespoons raw cane sugar

Put the raspberries in a blender or food processor and blend until smooth. Slowly add the simple syrup to taste, depending on the sweetness of the raspberries. Strain through a fine-mesh sieve into a bowl.

Slice the mango halves into fans.

Lay the cookies on a broiler pan. Set the fans on top of each cookie and sprinkle each with 1 tablespoon raw sugar. With a small blowtorch, caramelize the sugar. If you don't have a blowtorch, slide the broiler pan under a preheated broiler about 3 inches from the heat source to caramelize. Either way, watch the sugar closely; it will caramelize in about 1 minute.

Place each cookie on a dessert plate. Drizzle the raspberry coulis around the cookie on the plate.

NOTE: MANGOS ARE MESSY TO WORK WITH, AND IT MAY TAKE SOME PRACTICE BEFORE YOU CAN SUCCESSFULLY HALVE OR QUARTER THEM. EACH MANGO HAS TWO FLATTENED "FACES," FRONT AND BACK. CUT OFF THE FRUIT OF ONE FACE STRAIGHT DOWN NEXT TO THE LARGE FLAT SEED. CUT OFF THE OTHER FACE OF THE FRUIT. PEEL AWAY THE SKIN AND CUT OFF THE FRUIT ON THE BOTTOM, TOP, AND SIDES. FAN OR DICE THE MANGO.

cardamom shortbread

1⅓ cups (2⅔ sticks) unsalted butter
at room temperature

⅓ cup sugar

3 egg yolks

1 teaspoon pure vanilla extract

2½ cups all-purpose flour, sifted

2 teaspoons ground cardamom

⅛ teaspoon salt

In the bowl of an electric mixer set on medium-high speed, cream the butter and sugar for 3 to 4 minutes, or until light and fluffy. Add the egg yolks one at a time, beating well after each addition and scraping down the sides of the bowl as needed. Beat in the vanilla.

In another bowl, whisk the flour, cardamom, and salt together.

Reduce the mixer speed to medium-low and add the flour in a few additions until incorporated. Scrape the dough from the bowl and gather it into a mass. Wrap in plastic wrap and refrigerate for at least 1 hour or as long as overnight.

Preheat the oven to 350°F.

On a lightly floured surface, knead the chilled dough a few times to warm it up and make it pliable. With a floured rolling pin, roll it into a rectangle about ⅛ inch thick and 12 inches long. Using a small, sharp knife, cut the dough into the desired shapes. For the Champagne Mango and Raspberry Coulis recipe, cut the dough into 4-by-3-inch rectangles. Lay on an ungreased baking sheet and prick the shortbread several times with a fork. Bake for about 12 minutes, or until lightly browned and firm.

Transfer to wire racks to cool.

Desserts that don't rely on butter, cream, and eggs are challenging. Here, I debunk the theory that crème brûlée must be made with heavy cream and use milk instead. The secret weapon is sweet potato juice, which provides texture and an enticing flavor that is hard to pin down. This custard is not as thick as a classic French crème brûlée, but is more like the Spanish version, crema catalana. Restaurant chefs don't much like making crema catalana because it requires constant stirring at the stove. Be sure the custard gets thick enough— it's worth the effort.

sweet potato brûlée

SERVES 6

2 cups whole milk

½ cup raw cane sugar

½ vanilla bean, halved horizontally

8 large egg yolks

2 cups sweet potato juice (see page 166)

¼ teaspoon salt

Grated fresh nutmeg to taste

2 tablespoons Kentucky bourbon

In a small saucepan, combine the milk, ¼ cup of the sugar, and the vanilla bean. Bring to a simmer over medium heat. Cook, stirring occasionally, until the sugar dissolves. Do not let the milk boil. Strain through a fine-mesh sieve. Reserve the vanilla bean for another use.

Put the egg yolks in a double boiler and gradually whisk in the hot milk. Stir in the sweet potato juice and salt. Add the nutmeg.

Cook over simmering water for 30 minutes, stirring constantly, until the custard is as thick as soft pudding.

Preheat the oven to 300°F.

Strain the thickened custard through a fine-mesh sieve into a bowl. Ladle into six 8-ounce ramekins. Set the ramekins in a roasting pan and add hot water to come about halfway up the sides of the ramekins. Bake on the center rack of the oven for 30 minutes, or until set but not completely firm in the center.

CONTINUED

Remove from the oven and let the ramekins cool on wire racks. Cover with plastic wrap and refrigerate for about 2 hours, or until thoroughly chilled.

sweet potato brûlée

CONTINUED

Preheat the boiler or plan to use a kitchen blowtorch.

Sprinkle 2 teaspoons of the remaining cane sugar over each chilled custard. Slide the dishes under the broiler so that they are about 3 inches from the heat source and broil for about 1 minute, or run the blowtorch slowly over the sugar to melt and caramelize it. Watch carefully to prevent the sugar from burning.

Heat the bourbon in a small saucepan over medium heat just until warm. Pour 1 teaspoon bourbon over each custard and ignite it with a match. Serve immediately.

basics

creamy corn sauce 156

fire-roasted sweet pepper sauce 156

buttermilk sour cream 157

raw sugar simple syrup 157

red or golden beet syrup 157

rutabaga syrup 158

pear syrup 158

grilled corn 158

shelled fava beans 158

roasted garlic 159

roasted garlic cloves 159

roasted garlic stock 159

spring garlic stock 160

rich chicken stock 160

chicken glaze 161

rich beef or veal stock 161

ham hock stock 162

rich fish stock 162

roasted vegetable stock 163

simple vegetable stock 164

roasted corn stock 164

rich mushroom stock 165

huitlacoche sauce 165

juicing fruits and vegetables 166

roasting vegetables 166

When I opened Heartbeat, not being able to offer cream sauce, mayonnaise, or beurre blanc had me chewing my fingernails to the quick. I thought about one of my favorite dishes, a creamy corn succotash with a hint of vanilla. I also thought about crab cakes without mayonnaise and sauces that begged to be finished with butter. I started experimenting with sauces that, I reasoned, might thicken on their own when gently heated because they were made with a starchy vegetable juice. This sauce was one of my early successes. I found it thickened even further when refrigerated, which made it perfect for binding crab cakes (hooray!) and for salad dressings.

creamy **corn** sauce

MAKES ABOUT 1½ CUPS SAUCE

6 cups fresh corn kernels (about 12 large ears)

1 to 2 tablespoons fresh lemon juice (to taste)

Salt and freshly ground pepper to taste

Juice the kernels in a vegetable juicer. You should have 1½ to 2 cups corn juice.

Put the corn milk in a double boiler and heat over gently simmering water, stirring constantly to prevent simmering, for 4 to 6 minutes, or until thickened and smooth. If the sauce simmers, it may curdle. If you stop stirring, it may break and will not be retrievable.

Remove from the heat and strain through a fine-mesh sieve. Season with lemon juice, salt, and pepper.

Use now, or cover and refrigerate for up to 5 days. Use cold or warm. Warm the refrigerated sauce in a double boiler over simmering water, stirring constantly to prevent curdling, for 6 to 8 minutes.

This is a particularly versatile sauce that competes with sauces made with meat or poultry stock reductions, or even with butter. It takes a little patience and finesse, but once you put the ingredients in a double boiler, it's just a matter of waiting and adding water to the bottom of the double boiler as needed to protect the sauce. This can be used to finish other sauces, although it has exciting flavor on its own. This has a purity that you never get with a purée; it's far more striking. I use this like tomato sauce—it's splendid with fish and you can dress it up as you like. For instance, for dishes with Southwestern flavors, I add diced chilies.

fire-roasted **sweet pepper** sauce

MAKES ABOUT 3 CUPS

8 red bell peppers, roasted, peeled, and chopped (see page 104)

8 red bell peppers, seeded and juiced (see page 104)

Salt and freshly ground pepper to taste

In a double boiler, combine the chopped peppers and pepper juice and cook over simmering water for about 1½ hours, or until all the juice evaporates. Check the water level several times during cooking and add more if needed.

At this point, the coarse sauce will resemble thin tomato paste. Transfer to a blender or food processor and purée until smooth. Season with salt and pepper.

Use now, or cover and refrigerate for up to 3 days. Reheat gently over medium heat until nearly hot.

When you heat buttermilk until it curdles and then drain off the watery whey, the end result is this satisfying and rich alternative to sour cream.

buttermilk sour cream

MAKES ABOUT 1¾ CUPS

2 cups low-fat buttermilk

4 Roasted Garlic Cloves (page 159)

Salt and freshly ground pepper to taste

In a double boiler, combine the buttermilk and garlic. Cook over simmering water, without stirring, for 15 to 20 minutes, or until the milk solids curdle in the center of the pan and leave a ring of watery liquid around the rim.

Strain and discard the watery liquid. Transfer the curdled milk to a blender or food processor. Puree until smooth. Season with salt and pepper.

Use now, or cover and refrigerate for up to 4 days. Use as you would sour cream. If necessary for a recipe, reheat gently without boiling.

raw sugar simple syrup

MAKES ABOUT 1 CUP

2 cups raw cane sugar

1 cup water

In a small saucepan, stir the sugar and water together. Heat over medium-high heat until boiling. Reduce the heat slightly and cook, stirring, until the sugar dissolves and the syrup is clear.

Let cool to room temperature. Use now, or cover and refrigerate indefinitely. I like to keep simple syrup in a glass jar.

red or golden beet syrup

MAKES ABOUT ¼ TO ½ CUP

3 cups beet juice (see page 166)

Put the beet juice in a saucepan and set over medium heat. Bring to a simmer and skim the thick foam that rises to the surface.

Reduce the heat to low and simmer very gently for 30 to 45 minutes, skimming occasionally, until the juice reduces to the consistency of maple syrup.

Let cool to room temperature. Use now, or cover and refrigerate for up to 3 weeks.

rutabaga syrup

MAKES ABOUT ⅓ CUP

3 cups rutabaga juice (see page 166)

Put the rutabaga juice in a saucepan and set over medium heat. Bring to a simmer and skim the thick foam that rises to the surface.

Reduce the heat to low and simmer very gently for 30 to 45 minutes, skimming occasionally, until the juice reduces to the consistency of maple syrup.

Let cool to room temperature. Use now, or cover and refrigerate for up to 3 weeks.

pear syrup

MAKES ABOUT ⅓ CUP

3 cups pear juice (see page 166)

Put the pear juice in a saucepan and set over medium heat. Bring to a simmer and skim the thick foam that rises to the surface.

Reduce the heat to low and simmer very gently, skimming occasionally, for 30 to 45 minutes, or until the juice reduces to the consistency of maple syrup.

Let cool to room temperature. Use now or cover and refrigerate for up to 3 weeks.

grilled corn

Fresh ears of corn, husked

Light a fire in a charcoal grill or preheat a gas grill to medium. Lay the corn directly on the grill and cook for 6 to 8 minutes, turning frequently until lightly charred. Let the corn cool a little, and then slice the kernels from the cobs.

NOTE: SIX EARS OF CORN YIELD ABOUT 3 CUPS OF KERNELS.

shelled fava beans

It's easy to slit the bean pod open and remove the beans inside. What is tricky is removing the inner skin. I use my thumb to rip the top of the skin and then pop out the bean. It's time-consuming, but the season for fava beans is so short, you only do this several times every year.

Remove the beans from the outer shell. Bring a pot of water to a boil. Blanch in a pot of boiling water for 30 to 60 seconds. Drain and plunge the beans into ice water.

Lift the beans from the ice water and tear off the top of the bean with your thumbnail. Peel off the skin.

Garlic is usually harvested fully grown and sold as a multi-clove bulb or head, but it also comes in several other forms. In the early spring, green garlic shoots appear in the garden. Later in the spring, young bulbs take a more recognizable form as spring, or green, garlic, which can be harvested and appreciated for its fresh, mellow flavor. Before being harvested, spring garlic plants provide scapes, or leaves of sprouting young garlic. Nature dictates that these eventually bend to the ground, but before they droop earthward, the extravagantly pretty, curly, pale green shoots can be picked and simmered, sautéed, or grilled.

To find these kinds of garlic, visit local farm stands or farmers' markets. Let the farmers know you'll gladly buy spring garlic and garlic scapes. Buying directly from the farmer and voting with our dollars is a good way to return family farms to the prominence they once rightly enjoyed.

roasted garlic

1 or more garlic bulbs

Preheat the oven to 300°F. Peel the excess papery skin from the garlic bulb(s) but leave the cloves attached. Wrap the bulb in aluminum foil. Roast for 45 minutes to 1 hour, or until softened. Unwrap the garlic and let it cool to the touch. Squeeze the softened garlic pulp from the bulb(s).

NOTE: FOR 1 CUP OF ROASTED GARLIC PULP, ROAST 6 TO 8 HEADS OF GARLIC.

There is more than one way to roast garlic. Here's how to roast just a few cloves in a dry skillet (thank you, Mark Miller!).

roasted garlic cloves

Unpeeled garlic cloves, as needed

Put the cloves in a dry cast-iron skillet and cook over low heat for 20 to 30 minutes, or until softened. Turn frequently so that the cloves soften but do not brown. Slide the cloves from the skillet onto a plate to cool to the touch. Squeeze the softened garlic pulp from the individual cloves.

Using roasted garlic results in a deeply flavored, mellow stock.

roasted garlic stock

MAKES ABOUT **8** CUPS

1 cup roasted garlic pulp (6 to 8 heads), see above

**8 cups Rich Chicken Stock (page 160)
or Roasted Vegetable Stock (page 163)**

2 tablespoons minced fresh summer savory or rosemary

In a 3- to 4-quart saucepan, combine the garlic pulp and stock. Simmer gently, uncovered, over medium heat for 30 minutes.

Remove the pan from the heat and stir in the herb. Let stand for about 5 minutes, then strain through a fine-mesh sieve lined with 3 layers of dampened cheesecloth. Let cool. Use now, or cover and refrigerate for up to 3 days or freeze for up to 2 months.

I love the universal nature of garlic, which in turn seems to love everything you can imagine, with the exception of dessert (although some chefs have tried—and failed—to make it part of that course). When you make this, use the appropriate bones for the intended use. If you use it in a vegetarian dish, replace the bones with mushroom stems or your favorite roasted root vegetable. Replace the chicken stock with vegetable stock.

spring garlic stock

MAKES ABOUT **6** CUPS

1½ pounds garlic scapes (Egyptian garlic)

2 tablespoons grapeseed oil

2 pounds bones (fish for fish or seafood dishes, game for game dishes, veal for red meat, chicken for poultry)

10 bulbs spring (green) garlic

8 cups Rich Chicken Stock (page 160)

¼ cup freshly torn thyme leaves

Coat the scapes evenly with the oil. Heat a large sauté pan or skillet over medium-high heat and sear the scapes for 2 to 4 minutes, or until wilted and lightly browned.

In a large stockpot, combine the scapes, bones of your choice, garlic, and stock.

Bring to a simmer over medium heat. Reduce the heat to medium-low and simmer gently, uncovered, for 45 minutes. Add the thyme and simmer 3 minutes longer. Strain through a fine-mesh sieve lined with 3 layers of damp cheesecloth into a bowl. Let cool. Use now, or cover and refrigerate for up to 3 days or freeze for up to 2 months.

You will note that there is only one ingredient in this stock, other than water. I like the pure flavor of chicken and cool, clear water—use filtered water if you can. This way, the final esssence is not muddied with competing flavors of vegetables or herbs. Just chicken. I follow the same philosophy making all meat stocks: just bones and water. I suggest you buy bone-in chickens and bone them yourself. Store the bones in the freezer and use them to make stock. The bony chicken parts sold for stock tend to be very fatty.

rich chicken stock

MAKES ABOUT **4** CUPS

5 pounds chicken bones and bony chicken parts, trimmed of excess fat

Preheat the oven to 425°F.

Put the bones in 2 large roasting pans or deep baking pans. Do not crowd the pans. Roast for about 45 minutes, or until the bones are well browned. Turn the bones several times during roasting.

Transfer the bones to a stockpot large enough to hold them with about 6 inches of space in the pot above the bones. Add enough water to cover the bones by 1 inch. Bring to a full simmer over medium heat. Scoop about 2 cups of the simmering water from the pot and pour about 1 cup into each of the roasting pans. Swirl the water in the pans, stirring to scrape up the browned bits from the bottom of the pan. Return to the stock.

Stir off the foam that forms on the surface. It's important to keep the foam from simmering back into the stock, which will make it cloudy.

Reduce the heat to medium-low and simmer, uncovered, for 2½ hours, continuing to skim the foam and fat from the stock.

Strain through a sieve into a bowl. Line a fine-mesh sieve with 3 layers of dampened cheesecloth and strain the stock a second time. Measure the stock and pour into a clean saucepan. You should have about 8 cups.

Cook the stock, uncovered, over medium-high heat for about 30 minutes, or until reduced by half. Cool in an ice-water bath. Cover and refrigerate for up to 3 days or freeze for up to 2 months.

chicken glaze

MAKES ABOUT ½ CUP

4 cups Rich Chicken Stock (page 160)

In a pot, bring the stock to a boil over high heat. Reduce the heat and simmer the stock for 45 to 60 minutes, or until the consistency of maple syrup.

Use now, or let cool, cover, and refrigerate for up to 3 days. Reheat gently before using.

rich beef or veal stock

MAKES ABOUT 6 CUPS

10 pounds beef or veal bones, trimmed of excess meat and fat and cut into 2-inch pieces

Preheat the oven to 375°F.

Put the bones in 2 large roasting pans. Do not crowd the pans. Roast for about 1¼ hours, or until the bones are well browned. Turn the bones several times during roasting.

Transfer the bones to a stockpot large enough to hold them with about 6 inches of space in the pot above the bones. Add enough water to cover the bones by 1 inch. Bring to a full simmer over medium heat. Scoop about 2 cups of simmering water from the pot and pour about 1 cup into each of the roasting pans. Swirl the water in the pans, stirring to scrape up the browned bits from the bottom of the pan. Return to the stock.

Skim the foam that forms on the surface. It's important to keep the foam from simmering back into the stock, which makes it cloudy.

Reduce the heat to medium-low and cook at a low simmer for at least 8 hours, continuing to skim the foam and fat from the stock.

Strain the stock through a sieve into a bowl. Line a fine-mesh sieve with 3 layers of dampened cheesecloth and strain the stock a second time. Measure the stock for yield and pour into a clean saucepan. You should have about 5 cups.

Cook the stock, uncovered, over medium-low heat for about 30 minutes, or until reduced by half. Cool in an ice-water bath. Use now, or cover and refrigerate for up to 3 days or freeze for up to 2 months.

Ham hock stock may not sound healthful but as with any stock, careful skimming is key to making it as fat-free as possible. Attending to the skimming is a bore, but it's important for every stock—especially this one. Ham hocks give off more foam and fat than other bones, which means it's necessary to skim constantly. If you feel this might be more trouble than it's worth, don't despair. Ham hock stock is the best smelling of all, so enjoy the aroma while you skim!

ham hock stock

MAKES ABOUT **8** CUPS

5 pounds fresh ham hocks

5 pounds smoked ham hocks

Put the bones in a stockpot large enough to hold them with about 6 inches of space in the pot above the bones. You may need 2 pots. Add enough water to cover the bones by 1 inch. Bring to a full simmer over medium heat. Skim off the foam that forms on the surface. It's important to keep the foam from simmering back into the stock, which makes it cloudy.

Reduce the heat to medium-low and cook at a very low simmer for 5 hours, continuing to skim the foam and fat from the stock.

Remove from the heat and let the stock cool nearly to room temperature. This allows the hock meat to adhere better to the bone, so it's easier to strain the stock without bits of meat escaping through the sieve.

Strain through a sieve into a bowl. Line a fine-mesh sieve with 3 layers of dampened cheesecloth and strain

the stock a second time. Measure the stock for yield and pour into a clean saucepan. You should have about 4 quarts.

Cook the stock over medium-high heat for about 45 minutes, or until reduced by half. Cool in an ice-water bath. Use now, or cover and refrigerate for up to 3 days or freeze for up to 2 months.

This stock can be a little tricky, but is definitely worth the hassle. With chicken, veal, and pork, you enrich the stock by reducing it to concentrate the flavor. Fish stock can be reduced, but its flavors will not remain true; on the contrary, they become mysteriously muddy, depending on the fish used. I address this by making stock, and then pouring it over fresh bones and starting over. The result is fish stock that is rich and true in flavor.

rich fish stock

MAKES ABOUT **8** CUPS

10 pounds fish bones from white-fleshed fish like halibut, flounder, or sea bass

Rinse the bones thoroughly under cold running water. Use a vegetable brush to scrub the bones while washing them.

Transfer about half of the bones to a stockpot large enough to hold them with about 6 inches of space in the pot above the bones. Add enough water to cover the bones by 1 inch. Bring to a full simmer over medium heat. Skim off the foam that forms on the surface. It's important to keep the foam from simmering back into the stock, which will make it cloudy.

Reduce the heat to medium low and cook at a low simmer for about 45 minutes, continuing to skim the foam and fat from the stock.

Strain the stock through a sieve into a bowl. Let cool to room temperature.

Put the remaining 5 pounds of bones in a large stockpot and pour the stock over them. Cook, as directed above, for 45 minutes.

Strain the stock through a sieve into a bowl. Line a fine-mesh sieve with 3 layers of dampened cheesecloth and strain the stock a second time. Cool in an ice-water bath. Use now, or cover and refrigerate for up to 2 days or freeze for up to 1 month.

A good vegetable stock is just as significant as a good poultry or meat stock. Vary the character of the stock by choosing raw or cooked vegetables, not scraps. This rich stock is flavored by roasted vegetables (see page 166). Enhance its complexity further by reducing it to concentrate the flavor. This and the following recipe are two ways to make excellent vegetable stock.

roasted vegetable stock

MAKES ABOUT **2** QUARTS

8 ounces rutabagas, roasted

1 pound carrots, roasted

8 ounces turnips, roasted

8 ounces white onions, roasted

8 ounces parsley roots or parsley stems, roasted

Combine the ingredients in a stockpot large enough to hold them with about 6 inches of space at the top of the pot. Add cold water to cover by 1 inch.

Simmer the stock for 2 hours over medium heat. Strain through a fine-mesh sieve, pressing on the vegetables with the back of a large spoon to force out as much of the liquid as possible. Strain a second time through a fine-mesh sieve lined with 3 layers of dampened cheesecloth. Let cool. Use now, or cover and refrigerate for up to 1 week or freeze for up to 1 month.

simple vegetable stock

MAKES ABOUT **8** CUPS

1 cup chopped onion

1 cup chopped peeled turnips

⅔ cup chopped celery

1 cup chopped carrots

⅔ cup chopped fennel

⅔ cup chopped parsley roots or stems

Combine all the ingredients in a stockpot large enough to hold them with about 6 inches of space at the top of the pot. Add cold water to cover by 1 inch.

Simmer the stock for 2 hours over medium heat. Strain through a fine-mesh sieve, pressing on the vegetables with the back of a large spoon to force out as much of the liquid as possible. Strain a second time through a fine-mesh sieve lined with 3 layers of dampened cheese-cloth. Let cool. Use now, or cover and refrigerate for up to 1 week or freeze for up to 1 month.

This is great for chowder and fish stews.

roasted corn stock

MAKES ABOUT **4** CUPS

10 scraped corn cobs
(after kernels have been removed for juicing),
each cut into 3 pieces

2 tablespoons grapeseed oil

½ cup diced onion

4 cups water

Preheat the oven to 400°F.

Coat the corn cob pieces with oil and lay them on a baking sheet. Roast, turning occasionally, for about 30 minutes, or until browned. Sprinkle the onion over the cobs, spray with vegetable-oil cooking spray, and roast for about 7 minutes longer, or until the onion softens.

In a large stockpot, combine the cobs, onion, and water. Bring to a low simmer over medium-low heat and cook for 1 hour. Strain the broth through a fine-mesh sieve. Let cool. Use now, or cover and refrigerate for up to 1 week or freeze for up to 1 month.

rich mushroom stock

3 pounds mushroom stems and other scraps

Salt and freshly ground black pepper to taste

Preheat the oven to 350°F.

Spread the mushroom stems and scraps on an ungreased baking sheet. Roast for 20 to 30 minutes, or until lightly browned. Turn the mushrooms once or twice during roasting to promote even browning.

Transfer the mushrooms to a large stockpot and add enough cold water to cover the mushrooms by 2 inches. Bring to a boil over high heat, reduce the heat and simmer for about 1 hour.

Strain the broth through a fine-mesh sieve into a bowl. Press on the solids with the back of a spoon to extract as much liquid and flavor as possible. Discard the solids.

Return the broth to the pot and bring to a boil over high heat and cook for about 20 minutes until reduced by half.

Remove from the heat and season with salt and pepper. Cool in an ice-water bath. Use now or cover and refrigerate for up to 3 days or freeze for up to 2 months.

huitlacoche sauce

MAKES ABOUT **3** CUPS

1½ cups water

1 cup huitlacoche, see Glossary (page 169)

2 tablespoons Roasted Garlic (see page 159)

2 tablespoons sliced shallots

2 tablespoons freshly grated lime zest

Fresh lime juice

Salt and freshly ground pepper

½ cup chopped fresh cilantro

Put the water, huitlacoche, garlic, and shallots in a medium saucepan and set over medium heat. Bring to a low simmer and cook gently for 20 to 30 minutes, until the huitlacoche is soft enough to purée.

Transfer to a blender or food processor. Purée until smooth. Season with lime juice, salt, and pepper to taste. Add the cilantro and purée again until it is well incorporated. Use now or store in a squeeze bottle or glass container and refrigerate for up to a week.

WHEN YOU JUICE FRUITS AND VEGETABLES, buy more than you think you will need. The yield varies depending on the moisture content of a particular fruit or vegetable, the time of year it was harvested, where it was harvested, and how it was stored. The amounts below are approximate and may yield more than you need. That's fine. Drink any juice you don't use. I particulary love carrot juice and all fruit juices. Potato and squash juice aren't very tasty!

To prepare fruits and vegetables for juicing, wash them under cold running water and cut away any soft spots. You should scrub root vegetables lightly with a coarse pad or brush, but there is no need to peel them. Slice or cut fruits and vegetables into manageable sizes. You should remove large pits and seeds, but there is no need to scrape out all seeds or remove stems. The juicer will take care of this.

juicing fruits and vegetables

FOR 1 CUP OF JUICE

- **apples:** 1 pound
- **asparagus:** 1 pound
- **beets:** 15 ounces
- **carrots:** 1 pound
- **celery:** 15 ounces
- **cherries:** 1 pound, pitted
- **corn kernels:** 1 pound (about 3 cups; kernels from 6 or 7 ears)
- **English peas:** 1 pound (2 cups shelled)
- **fennel:** 12 ounces
- **golden beets:** 12 ounces
- **pears:** 1 pound
- **plums:** 1 pound
- **rutabagas:** 12 ounces
- **squash:** 1¼ pounds
- **sweet potatoes:** 1¼ pounds
- **Yukon gold potatoes:** 1¼ pounds

(AMOUNTS ARE APPROXIMATE)

TO PREPARE VEGETABLES FOR ROASTING, wash them first under cold running water. Scrub root vegetables with a coarse pad or brush rather than peeling them. So many nutrients exist in the skin, it's a shame to peel them away. Scrubbing tenderizes the skin and removes any root hairs, which could burn during roasting.

Rub the vegetables with water or grapeseed oil and season with salt and pepper. Lay them on a baking sheet and roast in a preheated 300°F oven (unless otherwise instructed) until tender.

The roasting time will vary because the moisture and starch content of every fruit and vegetable varies depending on how the fruit or vegetable was grown and stored.

roasting vegetables

APPROXIMATE ROASTING TIMES:

- **beets:** 20 to 30 minutes for baby beets, 45 to 60 minutes for medium beets
- **carrots:** 15 to 20 minutes for baby carrots, 30 to 40 minutes for medium carrots
- **onions:** 30 to 40 minutes
- **parsnips:** blanch in simmering water for 15 minutes, then roast for 15 to 20 minutes
- **pearl or cipollini onions:** 15 to 20 minutes
- **potatoes (white, purple, Yukon gold):** 15 to 20 minutes for wedges
- **radishes:** 15 minutes for small radishes, 25 minutes for large radishes
- **scallions:** 15 to 20 minutes
- **shallots:** 10 to 15 minutes
- **squash:** 20 to 25 minutes for wedges, 10 to 15 minutes for 1-inch cubes
- **sweet potatoes:** 15 minutes for wedges
- **turnips:** 8 to 12 minutes for baby turnips, 15 to 25 minutes for medium turnips

glossary

almond flour: Made from finely ground almonds, this can be found at specialty foods stores, natural foods stores, and some supermarkets. As with most nut flours, the mild taste it imparts to food comes as a pleasant surprise. Unlike wheat flour, it contains no gluten and cannot provide structure to baked goods, and so is relied on for flavor and texture only. It does not keep well, so buy it in small amounts and store it, covered, in the refrigerator for up to 1 month.

apricot nectar: Intensely flavored apricot juice. It's sold in most supermarkets.

black Thai rice: Extremely popular in Southeast Asia and parts of China, this is a variety of unmilled sticky rice with a dark hull that turns purply black when cooked. After long cooking—up to an hour and a half—it tastes nutty and sometimes slightly fruity. In Southeast Asia, it is often served sweetened; here, it is more apt to be served in salads and with vegetables. Look for it in Asian markets or order it by mail order (see page 171).

bonito: Also known as katsuo, this member of the tuna family is commonly used for sashimi. Bonito can be found in Japanese markets and some supermarkets.

bonito flakes: Flaked dried bonito is one of the essential ingredients for the Japanese seasoning and soup base called dashi. Dried bonito is also available in powdered form.

cardamom pods: Cardamom is an intensely flavored, aromatic spice related to ginger that is most commonly used in curries and baked goods. It is sold as seed-filled pods or ground. The ground spice is not as pungent as the grind you can make by grinding it yourself with a mortar and pestle or spice grinder. The entire pod or just the seeds can be ground. The choice depends on the recipe.

Champagne mangos: Champagne mangos are smaller than other mangos but otherwise resemble them. Look for them in the spring and summer in specialty produce markets and some supermarkets. Substitute regular mangos when necessary. When ripe, mangos will give slightly when pressed, similar to an avocado, and have a lovely fragrance.

cipollini onions: These small, flat white onions are similar to pearl onions and share their mild flavor. Peel before cooking.

corn shoots: These tender, mild shoots are difficult to find but if you can, use them. Otherwise, substitute pea shoots, mâche, or another tender green.

daikon: A large white radish, also known as the mooli or icicle radish, daikon is sold in Japanese markets, many greengrocers, and supermarkets across the country. Juicy, crisp, and mild, it is available year-round, but is best during the winter. The large white root, which somewhat resembles a fat carrot, should be stored in the refrigerator and used within 1 week.

daikon sprouts: Daikon radish sprouts are sold where other sprouts are sold. If you cannot find them, use other radish sprouts or any peppery sprout.

dashi flakes: A mixture of dried bonito flakes, kombu, and seasonings, dashi flakes can be mixed with liquid to make an instant soup base and are also used as a seasoning. They may be labeled *hom-dashi*.

edamame: These are fresh soybeans still in the shell. Fresh edamame require slightly shorter cooking than thawed frozen and are harder to find. The frozen product, sold in Asian markets and supermarkets in regions of the country with large Asian populations, is excellent.

epazote: This pungent herb with serrated leaves is used most often in Mexican cooking and sometimes sold in markets that sell Mexican or Latin-American food. It also grows wild in parts of the United States, where it is known as pigweed or wormseed.

Extra-Virgin O Lemon Oil: This brand of lemon-flavored oil is available in gourmet shops and by mail order. If you cannot find this or another lemon-flavored oil, substitute any high-quality extra-virgin olive oil.

fava beans: These shell beans resemble large lima beans and are covered with a bitter skin that must be removed by blanching and peeling prior to cooking the bean. Very young, tender fava beans do not need peeling.

fig syrup: This is a seedless puree of figs that can be used as a dessert topping or an ingredient in the dessert itself. It adds depth and a pleasing hint of sweetness to savory dishes, such as game. Although some large supermarkets may carry it, natural foods stores and gourmet markets are the best bets for finding it.

fish sauce: Made from fermented fish, this salty sauce has a pungent aroma and strong flavor. It is used throughout Southeast Asia as a condiment, much like soy sauce or tamari, and also as a seasoning. It is sold in Asian markets and many specialty foods stores, as well as in supermarkets in those regions of the country with large Asian populations. Thai fish sauce is known as nam pla; Vietnamese fish sauce is known as *nuac nam.*

fleur de sel: The most expensive salt, this is harvested by hand and is made from the crust that forms on the surface of some sea salts. It is used as a condiment to sprinkle on foods before eating.

fresh bay leaves: Fresh bay laurel leaves impart a lovely, sweet flavor that cannot be compared to the flavor of dried bay leaves. Bay laurel plants are easy to grow; they flourish inside and can be overwintered in most climates, and are increasingly sold alongside other fresh herbs. Use fresh basil leaves if you cannot find fresh bay leaves.

garam masala: This blend of Indian spices usually includes black pepper, mace, cinnamon, cumin, and nutmeg. Ordinarily, garam masala is added to a dish either just before or after it is finished cooking. The gourmet sections of some supermarkets carry garam masala, but the best kinds are found in Indian markets.

garlic scapes: These are the curly pale-green-to-white tops of young garlic plants. If you grow your own garlic, harvest the scapes when you see them in the spring and early summer. Otherwise, look for them at farmers' markets, greengrocers, and specialty foods stores. They are also called Egyptian garlic.

hazelnut flour: Finely ground hazelnuts, this flour is typically found in specialty foods markets and natural foods stores. It imparts a subtle, sweet flavor to foods. It does not keep well, so buy it in small amounts and refrigerate, covered, for up to 1 month.

heirloom tomatoes: These nonhybrid species tend to be better tasting than hybrids, but they are also more expensive and harder to find. Specialty farmers' markets or specialty produce markets carry them along with other heirloom produce. If a recipe calls for a particular heirloom tomato and you cannot find it, substitute another. Otherwise, use vine-ripened tomatoes of any kind.

huitlacoche: This mushroomlike fungus grows on ears of corn. It has an indescribable pungent, smoky flavor and aroma. Look for it in Latino markets, or see Mail-Order Sources on page 171.

kombu leaves: This sea vegetable, or kelp, is harvested as long olive-brown leaves and then dried. It is also known as konbu or sea tangle. Bright green young kombu leaves are called battera. Kombu is an essential ingredient in dashi.

lemongrass: A flavorful herb from Southeast Asia, lemongrass gives food a subtle lemon flavor. Fresh lemongrass is sold in Asian markets, greengrocers, gourmet markets, and increasingly in supermarkets, particularly those in regions with large Asian populations. Cut off the woody stalks and peel the white part before using.

mâche: A green leafy plant native to Europe, mâche is usually used as a salad green but also is sometimes steamed for a side dish. Use mâche within a day or two of purchase. Look for it in farmers' markets, specialty produce markets, and some supermarkets. Mâche is also known as corn salad, field salad, field lettuce, or lamb's lettuce.

Meyer lemons: Commonly believed to be a cross between a lemon and a mandarin orange, Meyer lemons taste slightly sweeter than regular lemons. They are also slightly rounder and smaller and have a yellow-orange tint and a thin skin. Grown in California, they are hard to find outside that state. Use mild grapefruit or regular lemons instead.

mirin: A mildly alcoholic, sweet rice wine, typically used in Japanese cooking to add flavor to many dishes, mirin can be found in Japanese markets, natural foods stores, and some large supermarkets. Look for *hon-mirin,* which is "true" mirin, and avoid *aji-mirin,* which contains additives.

miso: A soy product, miso is used as a seasoning and soup base in Japan. It is made by fermenting soybeans with a grain such as barley, rice, or wheat. Every region of Japan has its own version of miso, which can range in color from beige to dark brown. Yellow miso is considered an all-purpose seasoning; red miso is saltier. Pale "white" miso is somewhat sweet. Most misos are smooth and pastelike, although some are chunky.

mizuna: A light salad green with a mild, cabbagelike flavor, mizuna is native to Japan. It is recognizable by its long, feathery leaves, which are crisp and green when fresh. Specialty produce markets and Asian markets may carry mizuna. Avoid it if it has brown and wilting leaves.

panko: Coarse Japanese bread crumbs used for coating and battering fried foods in a variety of Japanese dishes, panko creates a delicious crunchy crust that complements seafood in particular. It's available in Asian markets and some larger supermarkets.

parsley roots: These long white roots resemble very thin parsnips. They are sold in farmers' markets, greengrocers, and specialty produce stores, as well as some upscale supermarkets.

pea shoots: Also called *dau miu,* pea shoots are the thin, crisp tops of the green pea plant. They taste like a cross between peas and spinach. These may be difficult to find, but you can locate them in Asian markets. If you cannot find pea shoots, use mâche instead.

pomegranate molasses: This sweet syrup is sold in Middle Eastern and specialty foods stores.

praline paste: A very sweet, rich nut paste sold in cans or jars in specialty foods stores and by mail order, a little praline paste goes a long way. Store it, covered, in the refrigerator for up to 1 month after opening.

raw cane sugar: Raw cane sugar is metabolized more slowly in the body than granulated sugar. Plus, by virtue of being less processed, it's kinder to the earth. Look for supermarket brands such as Dixie Crystals and Sugar in the Raw, or products labeled Florida Cane Sugar.

raz al hanout: This North African spice mixture is commonly used with rice, couscous, and stews. It contains crushed dried rosebuds, and usually peppercorns, cardamom, mace, nutmeg, and cinnamon as well. Look for it in Middle Eastern markets.

sambal olek: This all-purpose Southeast Asian chili sauce is made of chilies, brown sugar, and salt. Spices may be added. It's available in Indonesian markets and most Asian markets. Substitute any other kind of hot chili sauce.

sea salt: This salt, harvested from the sea, has a pleasingly strong taste and crystalline texture. It's available in coarse or fine texture. *See also* fleur de sel.

shiso leaves: Lemon-flavored leaves of the perilla plant, these are closely related to mint and basil and most often used in Japanese dishes. Use in salads or as a garnish. They are available in Asian markets, particularly those specializing in Japanese food. They also are known as Japanese basil.

Sichuan peppercorns: Also known as Chinese pepper or Szechuan pepper, Sichuan peppercorns are a mildly hot, pleasantly flavorful spice. Berries of the prickly ash tree, they aren't really peppercorns, despite the striking resemblance. Asian markets and gourmet markets carry this spice, as do many supermarkets.

silken tofu: Silken tofu, the softest tofu, is sold in blocks that commonly weigh anywhere from 12 to 16 ounces.

spring garlic: Spring, or green, garlic has a small white bulb with long green stems.

star anise: The segmented star-shaped seed pod of a Chinese evergreen has a flavor close to although more bitter than that of traditional anise. Look for it in Asian markets, specialty foods stores, and some supermarkets.

sumac: The berries of the sumac bush are sold dried or ground for use as a spice. Sumac complements seafood, poultry, and vegetables with a fruity yet sour flavor. Look for it in Middle Eastern stores.

tahini (sesame paste): This thick paste is used in traditional Middle Eastern dishes such as hummus and baba ghanoush. Store-bought tahini has a layer of oil on top of the paste in the jar and must be mixed before use. Many supermarkets carry tahini, as do Middle Eastern markets and natural foods stores.

tamari sauce: A dark soy sauce used as a condiment or dipping sauce, tamari has a more subdued and richer flavor, a darker color, and a somewhat thicker texture than other soy sauces. It's sold in Japanese and other Asian markets, natural foods stores, and supermarkets.

Thai chilies: Diminutive, extremely hot chilies with heat that holds on through the cooking process. They are also known as bird chilies, are either green or red, and measure about 1 inch long. Thai chilies are available in supermarkets and Asian markets. Substitute jalapeño, serrano, or pequín chilies.

tofu: Tofu, Japanese for "bean curd," is made from the curds of soy milk. Depending on its processing, tofu can be firm, semi-firm, or silken (also called soft). It is used in salads, stir-fries, soups, sauces, and many other dishes. Tofu should be used within 1 week of purchase and must be stored in water to cover, which should be changed daily. Drain tofu prior to cooking. It's available in supermarkets, natural foods stores, and Asian markets.

wasabi powder: Available in paste form or as a powder to mix with an equal amount of tepid water. After mixing with water, let it sit for 10 minutes so the flavor can develop. Buy wasabi powder in small amounts, as the flavor begins to fade as soon as it is opened. It's available from natural foods stores and Japanese markets.

white salmon: Although most salmon are pink-fleshed, a small percentage are white. This is not the result of the fish's diet, but is a natural occurrence of breeding. White salmon were at one time considered inferior and tossed back when caught. Today, they are prized by chefs and home cooks. If you see it, try it. It is subtly sweet and tender, and is at its best when cooked gently.

yuzu: A Japanese fruit, the yuzu looks like a small lemon with bumpy skin. It has lots of seeds and tastes intensely of citrus and minerals, but is not very acidic. Look for it in Japanese markets. If you can't find it, use lemons.

mail-order sources

ASIA MARKET
71½ MULBERRY STREET
NEW YORK, NY 10013
212-962-2028
nam pla, wasabi powder, Sichuan peppercorns, sambal olek, black Thai rice and panko.

CENTRAL BOEKI
55-30 46TH STREET
MASPETH, NY 11378
718-729-8966
dashi flakes, bonito flakes, kombu leaves, kombu battera, and yuzu.

INDIAN ROCK PRODUCE
530 CALIFORNIA ROAD
P.O. BOX 317
QUAKERTOWN, PA 18951
800-882-0512
cipollini onions, corn shoots, epazote, huitlacoche, Meyer lemons, mizuna, and shiso leaves.

O OLIVE OIL
1854 FOURTH STREET
SAN RAFAEL, CA 94901
415-460-6598
O Lemon Oil and specialty oils.

PARIS GOURMET
145 GRAND STREET
CARLSTADT, NJ 07072
201-939-5656
almond flour and praline paste.

SID WAINER
P.O. BOX 50240
NEW BEDFORD, MA 02745
508-999-6408
www.sidwainer.com
fig syrup, pomegranate molasses, specialty honey, vinegars, and oils.

index

a

Almonds
  Almond Polenta Cake with
    Orange Cream, 146–47
  Granola, 138
  grinding, 147
Apples, juicing, 166
Apricots, Steel-Cut Oatmeal
  with Mission Figs and, 135
Asian Pear Salad with Tamari
  Pecans and Maytag Blue
  Cheese, 33
Asparagus
  Grilled Asparagus, 122
  juicing, 166

b

Basmati and Black Rice Juk, 51
Beans
  Black-Eyed Pea Soup with
    Wilted Greens, 49
  Chicken and Grilled-Corn
    Succotash, 77
  Lightly Salted Edamame, 127
  Roasted Monkfish with
    Porcini Mushrooms and
    Fava Beans, 59
  shelled fava, 158
  Sweet Corn and Vegetable
    Chowder, 42–44
  White Bean Dip, 31
Beef
  Garlic-Grilled Strip Steak with
    Corn Béarnaise, 101
  Natural Beef Tenderloin with
    Wild Mushrooms and Yukon
    Gold Potatoes, 99–100
  Rich Beef Stock, 161
Beets
  juicing, 166
  Mustard-Roasted Tenderloin
    of Pork with Rutabaga and
    Golden Beets, 92–93

Red or Golden Beet Syrup, 157
  roasting, 166
Bell peppers
  Fire-Roasted Sweet Pepper
    Sauce, 156
  Grilled Summer Peppers with
    Fresh Bay Leaves, 120
  Marinated Venison Loin Steaks
    with Onions and Sweet
    Peppers, 104–5
Bison "Cube" Steak with
  Fresh Figs, 103
Black-Eyed Pea Soup with
  Wilted Greens, 49
Bok Choy, "Wok"-Charred, 129
Breakfast Vegetable Hash, 134
Buttermilk Sour Cream, 157

c

Cabbage, Napa, Roast Capon
  with Autumn Pears and, 84–85
Cakes
  Almond Polenta Cake with
    Orange Cream, 146–47
  Flourless Hazelnut Cakes
    with Chocolate Centers,
    144–45
  Cardamom Shortbread, 150
Carrots
  juicing, 166
  roasting, 166
Cauliflower, Caramelized, Cured
  Salmon with, 64–66
Celery
  juicing, 166
  Pan-Roasted Cod with Celery
    and Heirloom Potatoes, 67
Celery root
  Celery Root and Truffle Soup,
    53
  Sautéed Halibut with Celery
    Root and Truffle, 61
Champagne Mangos with
  Raspberry Coulis and
  Cardamom Shortbread, 149

Cheese
  Almond Polenta Cake with
    Orange Cream, 146–47
  Asian Pear Salad with Tamari
    Pecans and Maytag Blue
    Cheese, 33
  Oven-Roasted Tomatoes with
    Goat Cheese and Extra-
    Virgin Olive Oil, 23
  Pastel Omelet with Shiitake
    Mushrooms, Goat Cheese,
    and Fresh Herbs, 137
  Vegetable Lasagne, 116–17
Cherries
  Grilled Leg of Lamb with
    Cherries, Rhubarb, and
    Horseradish, 94–95
  juicing, 166
Chestnuts
  Heirloom Squash Dressing,
    82–83
  Heirloom Squash Soup with
    Roasted Chestnuts, 48
  roasting and peeling, 82–83
Chicken
  Chicken and Grilled-Corn
    Succotash, 77
  Chicken Glaze, 161
  Pan-Roasted Chicken with
    Heirloom Tomatoes and
    Fresh Bay Leaves, 78–79
  Pistachio-Roasted Poussin, 74
  Rich Chicken Stock, 160–61
  Roast Capon with Napa
    Cabbage and Autumn
    Pears, 84–85
  Roasted Chicken Breasts with
    Dinosaur Plum Sauce, 76
Chocolate Centers, Flourless
  Hazelnut Cakes with, 144–45
Chutney, Pomegranate-Date, 97
Coriander Breast of Duck with
  Sweet Potato Sauce, 88–90
Corn
  Chicken and Grilled-Corn
    Succotash, 77
  Corn Béarnaise, 101

Crab Cakes with Papaya and
  Jicama Salad, 70
Creamy Corn Sauce, 156
Grilled Corn, 158
juicing, 166
"Marshmallow" Corn, 123
Roasted Corn Stock, 164
Roasted Vegetables with
  Sweet Corn and Fire-
  Roasted Sweet Pepper
  Sauce, 115
Sautéed Scallops with
  Creamy Corn Sauce, 24
Sweet Corn and Vegetable
  Chowder, 42–44
Sweet Pea, Corn, and
  Mushroom Risotto, 113
Crab Cakes with Papaya and
  Jicama Salad, 70
Creamy Corn Sauce, 156
Cured Salmon with Caramelized
  Cauliflower, 64–66

d

Date-Pomegranate Chutney, 97
Dip, White Bean, 31
Dressing, Heirloom Squash, 82–83
Duck, Coriander Breast of, with
  Sweet Potato Sauce, 88–90

e

Edamame, Lightly Salted, 127
Eggplant
  grilling, 117
  Vegetable Lasagne, 116–17
Eggs
  Pastel Omelet with Shiitake
    Mushrooms, Goat Cheese,
    and Fresh Herbs, 137

f

Fat, role of, 13, 18
Fennel
  Grilled Prawns with Fennel
    and Onions, 71
  juicing, 166

Figs
   Bison "Cube" Steak with
      Fresh Figs, 103
   Fresh Figs with Semolina
      Toast and Rhododendron
      Honey, 142
   Steel-Cut Oatmeal with
      Apricots and Mission Figs,
      135
Fire-Roasted Sweet Pepper
   Sauce, 156
Fish
   Cured Salmon with
      Caramelized Cauliflower,
      64–66
   Fresh Tuna and Radish Salad
      with Wasabi Dressing, 38
   Miso Salmon with English
      Pea Sauce, 62
   Pan-Roasted Cod with Celery
      and Heirloom Potatoes, 67
   Rich Fish Stock, 162–63
   Sashimi of Fluke with Sweet
      Shrimp, 28
   Spicy Grilled Snapper with
      Ginger and Lemongrass,
      56–58
   Steamed Black Bass with
      Kombu Noodles and
      Mushroom Dashi, 69
Flourless Hazelnut Cakes with
   Chocolate Centers, 144–45
Fruits, juicing, 166

g
Game Bird Seasoning, 84
Garlic
   Garlic-Grilled Strip Steak with
      Corn Béarnaise, 101
   Garlic Mashed Potatoes, 124
   Garlic Wilted Spinach, 128
   kinds of, 159
   Pan-Toasted Garlic and
      Wilted Spinach Soup, 52
   Roasted Garlic, 159
   Roasted Garlic Cloves, 159
   Roasted Garlic Stock, 159

   Spring Garlic Stock, 160
Granola, 138
Gravy, Sweet Potato, 81
Greens
   Asian Pear Salad with Tamari
      Pecans and Maytag Blue
      Cheese, 33
   Black-Eyed Pea Soup with
      Wilted Greens, 49
   Roasted Root Vegetables and
      Baby Greens Salad, 35
   Roasted Vegetables with
      Sweet Corn and Fire-
      Roasted Sweet Pepper
      Sauce, 115
   Green Tomato Soup with
      Heirloom Tomatoes and
      Vidalia Onion Garnish, 47

h
Ham Hock Stock, 162
Hazelnuts
   Flourless Hazelnut Cakes
      with Chocolate Centers, 144–45
   Granola, 138
Heirloom Squash Dressing, 82–83
Heirloom Squash Soup with
   Roasted Chestnuts, 48
Heirloom Tomato Salad with
   Aged Balsamic Vinaigrette, 37
Heirloom Tomato Soup, 45
Huitlacoche Sauce, 165

j
Jicama and Papaya Salad, Crab
   Cakes with, 70
Juicers, 9–10
Juices, 166
Juk, Basmati and Black Rice, 51

k
Kombu Noodles, Steamed
   Halibut with Mushroom Dashi
   and, 69

l
Lamb
   Grilled Leg of Lamb with
      Cherries, Rhubarb, and
      Horseradish, 94–95
   Rack of Lamb with
      Pomegranate-Date
      Chutney, 96
Lasagne, Vegetable, 116–17
Lightly Salted Edamame, 127

m
Mangos, Champagne, with
   Raspberry Coulis and
   Cardamom Shortbread, 149
"Marshmallow" Corn, 123
Melons, Summer, with Ginger, 22
Miso Salmon with English Pea
   Sauce, 62
Mushrooms
   grilling, 117
   Natural Beef Tenderloin with
      Wild Mushrooms and Yukon
      Gold Potatoes, 99–100
   Pan-Roasted Quail with
      Peach and Porcini
      Mushroom Hash, 87
   Pastel Omelet with Shiitake
      Mushrooms, Goat Cheese,
      and Fresh Herbs, 137
   Rich Mushroom Stock, 165
   Roasted Monkfish with
      Porcini Mushrooms and
      Fava Beans, 59
   Roasted Vegetables with
      Sweet Corn and Fire-
      Roasted Sweet Pepper
      Sauce, 115
   Root Vegetable and Wild
      Mushroom Hash, 125
   Steamed Black Bass with
      Kombu Noodles and
      Mushroom Dashi, 69
   Sweet Pea, Corn, and
      Mushroom Risotto, 113
   Vegetable Lasagne, 116–17

Mustard-Roasted Tenderloin
   of Pork with Rutabaga and
   Golden Beets, 91–93

n
Natural Beef Tenderloin with
   Wild Mushrooms and Yukon
   Gold Potatoes, 99–100

o
Oats
   Granola, 138
   Steel-Cut Oatmeal with
      Apricots and Mission Figs,
      135
Omelet, Pastel, with Shiitake
   Mushrooms, Goat Cheese,
   and Fresh Herbs, 137
Onions, roasting, 166
Oysters, Fresh, with Ginger-
   Sake Mignonette, 30

p
Pancakes, Squash, with Fig
   Syrup, 133
Papaya and Jicama Salad, Crab
   Cakes with, 70
Parsnips, roasting, 166
Pastel Omelet with Shiitake
   Mushrooms, Goat Cheese,
   and Fresh Herbs, 137
Peach and Porcini Mushroom
   Hash, Pan-Roasted Quail
   with, 87
Pears
   Asian Pear Salad with Tamari
      Pecans and Maytag Blue
      Cheese, 33
   juicing, 166
   Pear Syrup, 158
   Roast Capon with Napa
      Cabbage and Autumn
      Pears, 84–85
Peas
   Chicken and Grilled-Corn
      Succotash, 77
   juicing, 166

Miso Salmon with English Pea Sauce, 62
Sweet Pea, Corn, and Mushroom Risotto, 113
Pecans, Tamari, 34
Pepper Marinade, 104
Pistachio-Roasted Poussin, 74
Plums
  juicing, 166
  Roasted Chicken Breasts with Dinosaur Plum Sauce, 76
Polenta Cake, Almond, with Orange Cream, 146–47
Pomegranate-Date Chutney, 97
Pork, Mustard-Roasted Tenderloin of, with Rutabaga and Golden Beets, 91–93
Potatoes
  Garlic Mashed Potatoes, 124
  juicing, 166
  Natural Beef Tenderloin with Wild Mushrooms and Yukon Gold Potatoes, 99–100
  Pan-Roasted Cod with Celery and Heirloom Potatoes, 67
  roasting, 166
Poussin, Pistachio-Roasted, 74
Prawns. See Shrimp

q

Quail, Pan-Roasted, with Peach and Porcini Mushroom Hash, 87

r

Rack of Lamb with Pomegranate-Date Chutney, 96
Radishes
  Fresh Tuna and Radish Salad with Wasabi Dressing, 38
  roasting, 166
Raspberry Coulis, Champagne Mangos with Cardamom Shortbread and, 149
Raw Sugar Simple Syrup, 157
Raz al hanout, 97
Red or Golden Beet Syrup, 157

Rhubarb, Grilled Leg of Lamb with Cherries, Horseradish, and, 94–95
Rice
  Basmati and Black Rice Juk, 51
  Sweet Pea, Corn, and Mushroom Risotto, 113
Rich Beet Stock, 161
Rich Chicken Stock, 160–61
Rich Fish Stock, 162–63
Rich Mushroom Stock, 165
Rich Veal Stock, 161
Risotto, Sweet Pea, Corn, and Mushroom, 113
Root Vegetable and Wild Mushroom Hash, 125
Rutabagas
  juicing, 166
  Mustard-Roasted Tenderloin of Pork with Rutabaga and Golden Beets, 91–93
  Rutabaga Syrup, 158

s

Salads
  Asian Pear Salad with Tamari Pecans and Maytag Blue Cheese, 33
  Crab Cakes with Papaya and Jicama Salad, 70
  Fresh Tuna and Radish Salad with Wasabi Dressing, 38
  Heirloom Tomato Salad with Aged Balsamic Vinaigrette, 37
  Roasted Root Vegetables and Baby Greens Salad, 35
Sambal Barbecue Sauce, 56
Sashimi of Fluke with Sweet Shrimp, 28
Sauces
  Asian, 17
  Corn Béarnaise, 101
  Creamy Corn Sauce, 156
  without fat, 17–18

Fire-Roasted Sweet Pepper Sauce, 156
French, 11, 17
Huitlacoche Sauce, 165
Sambal Barbecue Sauce, 56
Squash Sauce, 110
Sweet Potato Sauce, 88
Tahini Sauce, 66
Sautéing, low-temperature, 78
Scallions, roasting, 166
Scallops
  Sautéed Scallops with Creamy Corn Sauce, 24
  Tamari Shrimp and Scallops, 27
Seasons, cooking with, 18–19
Seeds, toasting, 85
Shallots, roasting, 166
Shortbread, Cardamom, 150
Shrimp
  Grilled Prawns with Fennel and Onions, 71
  Sashimi of Fluke with Sweet Shrimp, 28
  Tamari Shrimp and Scallops, 27
Simple Vegetable Stock, 164
Soups
  Basmati and Black Rice Juk, 51
  Black-Eyed Pea Soup with Wilted Greens, 49
  Celery Root and Truffle Soup, 53
  Green Tomato Soup with Heirloom Tomatoes and Vidalia Onion Garnish, 47
  Heirloom Squash Soup with Roasted Chestnuts, 48
  Heirloom Tomato Soup, 45
  Pan-Toasted Garlic and Wilted Spinach Soup, 52
  Sweet Corn and Vegetable Chowder, 42–44
Sour Cream, Buttermilk, 157
Spices, toasting, 85
Spinach
  Garlic Wilted Spinach, 128
  Pan-Toasted Garlic and Wilted Spinach Soup, 52

Spring Garlic Stock, 160
Squash
  Heirloom Squash Dressing, 82–83
  Heirloom Squash Soup with Roasted Chestnuts, 48
  juicing, 166
  roasting, 166
  Squash Pancakes with Fig Syrup, 133
  Squash Sauce, 110
Steel-Cut Oatmeal with Apricots and Mission Figs, 135
Stocks
  Ham Hock Stock, 162
  Rich Beef Stock, 161
  Rich Chicken Stock, 160–61
  Rich Fish Stock, 162–63
  Rich Mushroom Stock, 165
  Rich Veal Stock, 161
  Roasted Corn Stock, 164
  Roasted Garlic Stock, 159
  Roasted Vegetable Stock, 163
  Simple Vegetable Stock, 164
  Spring Garlic Stock, 160
Succotash, Grilled-Corn, and Chicken, 77
Summer Melons with Ginger, 22
Sweet Corn and Vegetable Chowder, 42–44
Sweet Pea, Corn, and Mushroom Risotto, 113
Sweet potatoes
  juicing, 166
  roasting, 166
  Sweet Potato and Root Vegetable Gratin, 108
  Sweet Potato Brûlée, 151–53
  Sweet Potato Gravy, 81
  Sweet Potato Sauce, 88
Syrups
  Pear Syrup, 158
  Raw Sugar Simple Syrup, 157
  Red or Golden Beet Syrup, 157
  Rutabaga Syrup, 158

t

Tahini Sauce, 66

Tamari Pecans, 34

Tamari Shrimp and Scallops, 27

Tomatoes

Green Tomato Soup with
Heirloom Tomatoes and
Vidalia Onion Garnish, 47

Heirloom Tomato Salad with
Aged Balsamic Vinaigrette,
37

Heirloom Tomato Soup, 45

Oven-Roasted Tomatoes with
Goat Cheese and Extra-
Virgin Olive Oil, 23

Pan-Roasted Chicken with
Heirloom Tomatoes and
Fresh Bay Leaves, 78–79

Vegetable Lasagne, 116–17

Truffles

Celery Root and Truffle Soup,
53

Sautéed Halibut with Celery
Root and Truffle, 61

Turkey, Roast, with Sweet
Potato Gravy and Heirloom
Squash Dressing, 80–81

Turnips, roasting, 166

V

Veal Stock, Rich, 161

Vegetables. *See also* individual
vegetables

Breakfast Vegetable Hash, 134

juicing, 166

Roasted Root Vegetables and
Baby Greens Salad, 35

Roasted Vegetable Stock, 163

Roasted Vegetables with
Sweet Corn and Fire-
Roasted Sweet Pepper
Sauce, 115

roasting, 166

Root Vegetable and Wild
Mushroom Hash, 125

Simple Vegetable Stock, 164

Sweet Corn and Vegetable
Chowder, 42–44

Sweet Potato and Root

Vegetable Gratin, 108

Vegetable Lasagne, 116–17

Winter Vegetable Stew, 110–12

Venison Loin Steaks, Marinated,
with Onions and Sweet
Peppers, 104–5

W

Wasabi Dressing, 38

White Bean Dip, 31

Winter Vegetable Stew, 110–12

"Wok"-Charred Bok Choy, 129

y

Yogurt

draining, 48

Granola, 138

table of equivalents

The exact equivalents in the following tables have been rounded for convenience.

liquid/dry measures

U.S.	METRIC
1/4 teaspoon	1.25 milliliters
1/2 teaspoon	2.5 milliliters
1 teaspoon	5 milliliters
1 tablespoon (3 teaspoons)	15 milliliters
1 fluid ounce (2 tablespoons)	30 milliliters
1/4 cup	60 milliliters
1/3 cup	80 milliliters
1/2 cup	120 milliliters
1 cup	240 milliliters
1 pint (2 cups)	480 milliliters
1 quart (4 cups, 32 ounces)	960 milliliters
1 gallon (4 quarts)	3.84 liters
1 ounce (by weight)	28 grams
1 pound	454 grams
2.2 pounds	1 kilogram

length

U.S.	METRIC
1/8 inch	3 millimeters
1/4 inch	6 millimeters
1/2 inch	12 millimeters
1 inch	2.5 centimeters

oven temperature

FAHRENHEIT	CELSIUS	GAS
250	120	1/2
275	140	1
300	150	2
325	160	3
350	180	4
375	190	5
400	200	6
425	220	7
450	230	8
475	240	9
500	260	10